ILLUSTRATED LIBRARY OF COOKING

VOLUME 4 Cak-Can

Included here: *a full complement of cakes baked from scratch plus everything you need to know about filling, frosting and decorating cakes for every kind of occasion ... plus shortcut masterpieces created from store-bought cakes ... plus a whole chapter of luscious candies ... PLUS inventive recipes built entirely upon canned foods.*

ROCKVILLE HOUSE PUBLISHERS, INC.
ROCKVILLE CENTRE, NEW YORK 11570

Family Circle.

Illustrated Library of

COOKING

YOUR READY REFERENCE FOR A LIFETIME OF GOOD EATING

Picture Credits:
Best Foods, a Division of CPC International ● Blue Bonnet Margarine ● General
Mills ● Peanut Growers of Georgia and Alabama ● Planters Peanut Oil

Classy convenient foods gone classic: snow-drifted Valentine Alaska (Cakes to Buy and Build Upon, this volume): from other volumes: a molded cranberry crown, pumpkin tarts and a cream-ruffed cherry pie.

Table of Contents

CAKE BAKER'S ART

CAKE BAKER'S ART:
THE BASICS OF CAKE MAKING, SIMPLE SECRETS OF FROSTING THE CAKE, SPECIAL OCCASION CAKES, HOW TO DECORATE CAKES

Not so long ago, a woman's cooking ability was determined by the cakes she baked. And in some communities it still is, communities where state and county fairs are *the* events of the year. Judging time is a time of suspense and hope for champion cake bakers as they watch each cake being cut, poked, prodded, scrutinized and, of course, sampled. Each contestant crossed fingers that her entry would wear the blue ribbon; for her recipe, more than likely, was an old family favorite, perfected down the years, made with the very best the farm has to offer—home-churned butter, pale and sweet, just-gathered eggs, rich whole milk, foaming in its pail. Her cake was feathery, fine-grained, moist and meltingly tender. And of incomparable flavor.

Such cakes can still be made although the temptation is simply to whip up a mix because mixes are so very easy, available and good. Lately, however, a "back-to-scratch" movement appears to be gathering strength across America because young women, brought up on box cakes, are longing for personal contact with the raw materials of cooking, for participation and for the sense of pride that accompanies it. For them, and, indeed, for every woman who would try her hand at baking a cake the old-fashioned way, we have collected here the very best cake recipes that FAMILY CIRCLE has come across—velvety-crumbed butter cakes, billowy sponge and angel cakes, devastatingly rich chocolate cakes, heady spice cakes and gingerbreads together with the frostings and fillings that crown them with perfection.

 Cinnamony, rich and moist Banana-Nut Cake, filled and frosted with fluffy Rum Butter Cream Frosting.

THE BASICS OF CAKE MAKING

A cake you have baked yourself, and served to your family and friends with a glow of understandable pride, is a joy to all. To achieve the perfection that will give you many a happy baking day, you need only follow the simple tips and use the basic tools, ingredients and methods explained below.

TIPS FOR EASY BAKING

1. Read recipe through.
2. Assemble ingredients, making no substitutions.
3. Preheat the oven so it's ready for your cake.
4. Measure carefully.
5. Follow instructions for mixing.
6. Use baking pan specified, or its alternate (*see chart that follows*).
7. Bake and cool cake, following instructions exactly.

ABOUT MEASURING

Ingredients for many other recipes are somewhat flexible, but for cakes it is absolutely necessary that you follow the kinds and amounts of ingredients specified if you are to have success. Using the right tools gets you off to a good start. Just any old cup and any old kitchen spoon may work sometimes, but standard measuring tools are sure-fire. There are two kinds of measuring cups.

Liquid: Which may be found in 1-cup, 2-cup, and 4-cup measures, have a space at the top of the cup to allow for full measurement, but no spilling, when you are moving the cup.

Dry: Which are nested in sets from ¼ cup to 1 cup, make it easy to level off ingredients flush with rim.

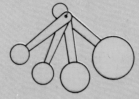

Measuring spoons: Are found in sets with measures from ¼ teaspoon to 1 tablespoon. They are simple to use, by dipping into baking powder, or spices, and leveling off.

Kinds of pans: Cake pans are made in standard sizes, and most are marked by size on the bottom. You may substitute one size for the other in most cakes (*see chart that follows*). However, the baking time may vary slightly. The most popular cake pans used are:

Round—
8 and 9 inch

Square—
8 and 9 inch

Bundt tube pan—
9 inch

Angel cake
tube pan—
9 and 10 inch

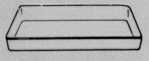

Oblong—13x9x2 inch

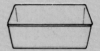

Loaf—9x5x3 inch

To be sure your cake pans are the diameter and depth called for in recipe, measure with a ruler.

ALTERNATE PAN CHART

If Your Recipe Calls For:	You May Use:
Three 8x1½-inch round pans	Two 9x9x2-inch square pans
Two 9x1½-inch round pans	Two 8x8x2-inch square pans OR One 13x9x2-inch oblong pan
One 9x5x3-inch loaf pan	One 9x9x2-inch square pan

Preparing pans: Use a generous coating of vegetable shortening (unless otherwise specified) and a light dusting of flour for an even, golden crust. For baking a cake in a pan with an odd shape: Fill pan ⅔ full with batter for our conventional butter cakes and ½ full for quick bowl cakes. For foam cakes, pans are *never* greased, since the airy cake batter needs to cling to the sides of the pan as it expands.

THE RIGHT INGREDIENTS

Cake flour is used in all recipes unless otherwise specified.
Shortening: Soft shortening, as called for in some recipes, is found in one- and three-pound cans.
Vegetable oil is used only in Chiffon cakes.
Butter or margarine (not whipped or diet) comes in the handy stick form.
Baking powder: Double-action is used in all recipes.
Eggs: Recipes tested with large eggs.

METHODS OF MIXING

Our butter cakes are made either by EASY CREAMING METHOD or QUICK BOWL METHOD. Both of the methods are possible by the use of the electric mixer. Whether you have a hand mixer or a standard mixer, all the laborious creaming is done for you in a few minutes with the whirling beaters.
If you should wish to make your cakes completely by hand, here's how:

For *EASY CREAMING METHOD:*
Add sugar slowly to the softened butter, margarine, or shortening; beat with wooden spoon until creamy. Add eggs, one at a time, beating until fluffy and light.

For *QUICK BOWL METHOD:*
Add shortening and part of liquid to bowl with dry ingredients. Beat with spoon 300 strokes. Add remaining liquid, eggs, and flavoring; beat another 300 strokes.

WHERE TO PUT PANS IN OVEN

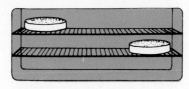

When baking two layers, place rack in center of oven, layers in opposite corners.

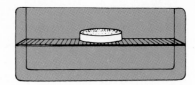

When baking one layer or an oblong, place in center of rack.
When baking three or four layers, use two racks in center third of oven. Stagger pans in opposite corners of both racks so they do not block heat circulation in oven.
For a tube cake, lower rack to bottom third of oven. Place pan in center.

HOW TO COOL CAKES

Cool foam cakes upside down over bottle until cold. (Don't worry, the cake won't fall out.) This keeps your cake high and light until the delicate walls are cool enough to support the weight of the cake.
Cool butter cakes on wire racks to allow air to circulate around hot cake.

WHEN CAKE IS DONE

The best of ovens sometimes vary in temperature. Therefore, you need some way of know-

393

ing when your cake is done. Here are three ways:

1 Follow time given in recipe *plus* your judgment.

2 Notice that baked cake shrinks slightly from sides of pan. (Not foam cakes.)

3 Touch center of cake lightly with fingertip. If baked, the top will spring back to shape; if not baked, imprint will remain.

FROSTING THE CAKE

An easy way to frost a cake is to put the cake plate on something you can turn. Place cake plate on a large bowl or sugar canister, then turn as you frost. Of course, if you have a lazy Susan, that is even better. Now ready to frost.

1 First, brush off all the loose crumbs.

2 For layer cakes, frost cakes with flat (*bottom*) sides together. Cake will be even and steady.

3 Frost entire outside of assembled cake with a *very thin* layer of frosting and let it set about 20 minutes. The thin coating holds crumbs in place and keeps them from mixing with the final frosting.

4 Frost sides of cake first, then frost top, swirling frosting for that grand finale.

Simple secrets

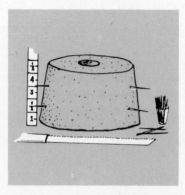

If a layer humps a bit in the center, shave off flat with a sharp knife. Brush any loose crumbs from edge with a pastry brush so they won't muss frosting, or you may prefer to trim a thin slice from edges.

To split an angel or chiffon cake into even layers, measure first, then mark your cutting lines with wooden picks. For cutting, use a serrated long-blade knife with a sawing motion to prevent tearing cake.

Have trouble with layers scooting apart after they're filled? Just anchor them in place with long thin metal skewers, and when top of cake is finished, take them out and smooth frosting over the tiny holes.

Pretty trims

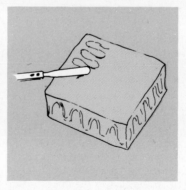

For this hobnail pattern, give cake a thick coat of frosting first, then press tip of spatula against frosting and pull outward quickly. Placing cake on a stemmed server for easy turning speeds the job.

This professional design proves how easy it is to be an artist. Using a spatula, draw a sweeping S in rows across frosting to give effect of softly shirred chiffon. Decorate sides with an up-and-down motion.

Meringue rosettes are simple to make with a teaspoon if you don't have a pastry bag. Depending on the size rosette you want, spoon up a bit of meringue, then drop into place, swirling upward to a peak.

A fruit cake crown dressed for Christmas. Trimmings are sugared mandarin oranges, citron, red cherries.

FROSTING TRIMS—PRETTY AND FAST

Everyday kitchen tools—knife, fork, teaspoon, strainer—a lacy doily, and a decorate-like-magic icing are your simple keys to these dressed-up toppers. Creamy butter frostings—your own or from a mix—make the deep swirls and line designs shown. The others are even easier.

Feathertop—Frost cake all over with white frosting, then drizzle melted chocolate in thin lines, about an inch apart, across top. Draw knife through frosting and across the chocolate to make this wavy featherlike pattern.

Icicles—A simple sugar-water frosting just thin enough to pour from a spoon is your doll-up secret here. Spoon the frosting over top of cake, letting it drip down around edge and inside the tube. Ring top with nuts.

Hopscotch—Frost oblong or square cake smoothly and let set until almost firm. Mark off evenly into squares with knife, then, with tines of fork, press lines in each square, alternating their direction.

Snowflake—A pretty lacy doily is your "decorator" here. Place doily upon an unfrosted cake, then fill a tea strainer with 10X (confectioners' powdered) sugar and tap out thickly and evenly over the top. Lift doily off.

396

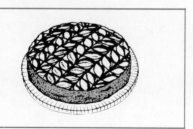

Swirlicues—Spread a thick frosting over top. (It doesn't have to be smooth.) With tip of knife, draw straight lines through it, reversing direction each time. The knife will pull the frosting just enough.

Birthday-bright—Out of candle-holders? Make your own with ready-to-press-out frosting from a pressurized can. Using the flower tip, pipe out frosting in lines, as shown, then finish off with tiny rosettes.

A sky-high, three-layer butter cake, blanketed with snowy frosting and garnished with sticks of pineapple.

TIPS FOR STORING AND FREEZING CAKES

Bake your cakes when you have the creative urge and then store or freeze them for later serving.

Be sure your cakes are completely cooled before storing or freezing.

To store cakes: Cover any cut surfaces with wax paper to keep moist. Cakes can be stored in a cake keeper or with a large bowl inverted over cake on serving plate for several days.

To freeze cakes: Unfrosted cakes freeze best and will store in freezer for up to 4 months. Simply wrap cakes in aluminum foil, transparent wrap, or in plastic bags and freeze. They will thaw in about 1 hour at room temperature. Frosted cakes, too, can be frozen but they should be frozen on a piece of cardboard or a cooky sheet until firm, then wrapped in aluminum foil, transparent wrap, or very large plastic bags. They will keep about 3 months. Thaw at room temperature for 2 hours.

BUTTER CAKES

The family of Butter Cakes is so called because butter was the original shortening used in these cakes in Colonial days. Later, margarines and vegetable shortenings entered the market and now all three are used with perfect results.

EASY CREAMING METHOD CAKES

What versatility! You can bake it as layers to frost with favorite icing, as a square to top with warm fruit sauce, or as cupcakes for lunch-box treats. It's a basic recipe every beginner cook should have in her file.

●

Basic Two-Egg Butter Cake
Bake at 350° for 30 minutes for layers, 40 minutes for square loaf and 25 minutes for cupcakes. Makes two 8-inch layers, or one cake, 9x9x2, or 24 cupcakes

2 cups sifted cake flour
2½ teaspoons baking powder
½ teaspoon salt
2 eggs, separated
½ cup (1 stick) butter or margarine, softened
1 cup sugar
1 teaspoon vanilla
¾ cup milk

1 Sift cake flour, baking powder, and salt onto waxed paper. Beat egg whites until they form soft peaks in a small bowl; then, with same beater, in a large bowl, cream butter or margarine, slowly adding sugar and beating until fluffy.
2 Beat in egg yolks and vanilla. Add flour mixture, ⅓ at a time, alternately with milk, beating just until blended. Fold in beaten whites. Pour into greased, wax-paper-lined 8x1½-inch layer pans, a 9x9x2 pan, or 24 muffin pans.
3 Bake in moderate oven (350°) 30 minutes for layers, 25 minutes for cupcakes, or 40 minutes for square. When cake is done, top will spring back when lightly pressed with finger. Cool in pan 5 minutes, turn out on racks to cool. Fill and frost as desired.

Pound Cake

Bake at 350° for 60 minutes. Makes one 9-inch tube cake

2⅓ cups sifted cake flour
1 teaspoon baking powder
½ teaspoon salt
⅔ cup butter or margarine, softened
1¼ cups sugar
3 eggs
½ cup milk
1 teaspoon grated lemon rind
1 tablespoon lemon juice

1 Grease a 9-inch tube pan; dust lightly with flour, tapping out any excess flour.
2 Sift flour, baking powder, and salt onto wax paper; reserve.
3 Combine butter or margarine, sugar and eggs in large bowl of mixer; beat at high speed 3 minutes. Remove bowl from mixer.
4 Combine milk, lemon rind, and juice in a cup. Stir in flour mixture alternately with milk mixture, beating after each addition until batter is smooth. Pour into prepared pan.
5 Bake in moderate oven (350°) 60 minutes or until center springs back when lightly pressed with fingertip. Cool 10 minutes on wire rack; loosen around edge and tube with a knife; turn out onto wire rack; cool completely.

Ruth Dove's Coconut Pound Cake

Bake at 325° for 1 hour and 15 minutes. Makes two 9x5x3-inch loaves

4 cups sifted cake flour
10 eggs, separated
2 cups (4 sticks) butter or margarine
2 cups sugar
1 tablespoon vanilla
½ cup flaked coconut, chopped

1 Grease two 9x5x3-inch loaf pans; dust lightly with flour; tap out any excess.
2 Beat egg whites until foamy-white and double in volume in a medium-size bowl; beat in ¼ cup sugar, 1 tablespoon at a time, until meringue stands in firm peaks.
3 Beat butter or margarine, remaining 1¾ cups sugar, and egg yolks in large bowl of mixer at high speed for three minutes. Stir in vanilla.
4 Sift in flour, stirring with a spoon or beating with mixer at low speed, just until blended. Fold in meringue; stir in coconut. Pour into prepared pans, dividing evenly.
5 Bake in slow oven (325°) 1 hour and 15 minutes, or until centers spring back when lightly pressed with fingertip.
6 Cool cakes in pans on wire racks 10 minutes. Loosen around edges with knife; turn out onto racks; cool completely. For easier slicing, wrap cooled cake in foil or transparent wrap and store overnight.

Frosty Coconut Cake (1-2-3-4 Cake)

Bake at 350° for 30 minutes. Makes three 8-inch layers

3 cups sifted cake flour
2 teaspoons baking powder
½ teaspoon salt
1 cup (2 sticks) butter or margarine, softened
2 cups sugar
4 eggs
1 teaspoon vanilla
1 cup milk
1 cup raspberry jam
DOUBLE-BOILER FROSTING (recipe follows)
1 cup flaked coconut

1 Grease three 8x1½-inch layer cake pans; dust lightly with flour; tap out any excess.
2 Sift flour, baking powder, and salt onto wax paper; reserve.
3 Beat softened butter or margarine, sugar, eggs, and vanilla in large bowl of mixer at high speed 3 minutes.
4 Beat in flour mixture alternately with milk, at low speed on mixer. Scrape sides of bowl with rubber scraper after each addition. Pour batter into prepared pans.

398

5 Bake in moderate oven (350°) 30 minutes, or until centers spring back when lightly pressed with fingertip.
6 Cool layers in pans on wire racks 10 minutes; loosen around edges with a knife; turn out onto wire racks; cool completely.
7 Split each layer in half to make 6 thin layers. Spread five of these layers with raspberry jam; stack layers, ending with plain layer. Frost side and top with DOUBLE-BOILER FROSTING; sprinkle coconut. Decorate top of cake with additional jam, if you wish.

Double Boiler Frosting

Makes enough to fill and frost three 8-inch layers

1½ cups sugar
¼ cup water
2 egg whites
2 tablespoons light corn syrup
1 teaspoon vanilla
¼ teaspoon salt

1 Combine all ingredients in top of a double boiler; beat until blended.
2 Place over simmering water; cook, beating constantly at high speed with an electric hand mixer or rotary beater, about 7 minutes, or until mixture triples in volume and holds firm peaks. Remove from heat.

Lord Baltimore Cake
(Gold Cake)

Bake at 350° for 30 minutes. Makes two 9-inch layers

Towering Frosty Coconut Cake, filled with ruby-hued raspberry jam, frosted and covered with flaky coconut.

A golden pound cake, baked in a crown mold, then for a party touch, drizzled with a thin see-through icing.

399

Party-cake, party-cake, swirled with snowiest icing, then scattered with a ring of mellow, minced pecans.

2 cups sifted cake flour
2½ teaspoons baking powder
¾ teaspoon salt
1 cup sugar
⅓ cup soft shortening
4 egg yolks
1 teaspoon vanilla
1 cup milk
    WHITE MOUNTAIN CREAM FROSTING (recipe follows)
    LORD BALTIMORE FILLING (recipe follows)

1 Grease two 9x1½-inch layer-cake pans; dust lightly with flour; tap out any excess.
2 Sift flour, baking powder, and salt onto wax paper; reserve.
3 Beat sugar, shortening, egg yolks, and vanilla in large bowl of mixer at high speed 3 minutes. Remove bowl from mixer.
4 Stir in flour mixture alternately with milk, beating after each addition until batter is smooth. Pour batter into prepared pans.
5 Bake in moderate oven (350°) 30 minutes, or until centers spring back when lightly pressed with fingertip.
6 Cool layers in pans on wire racks 10 minutes; loosen around edges with a knife; turn out onto wire racks; cool completely.
7 Put layers together with LORD BALTIMORE FILL-ING; frost side and top with remaining WHITE MOUNTAIN CREAM FROSTING.
8 Decorate with pecan halves and cherry halves, if you wish.

White Mountain Cream Frosting
Makes enough to fill and frost two 9-inch layers

1 cup sugar
⅓ cup light corn syrup
¼ cup water
¼ teaspoon salt
4 egg whites
⅛ teaspoon cream of tartar
½ teaspoon vanilla

1 Combine sugar, corn syrup, water, and salt in a small saucepan; cover. Heat to boiling; uncover; boil gently until mixture registers 242° on a candy thermometer, or until a small amount of the hot syrup falls threadlike from spoon.
2 While syrup cooks, beat egg whites with cream of tartar in a large bowl until stiff peaks form when beaters are removed. Pour hot syrup onto egg whites in a very thin stream, beating all the time at high speed until frosting is stiff and glossy. Beat in vanilla.
    PINK MOUNTAIN CREAM FROSTING: Follow above recipe using ¼ cup maraschino cherry liquid in place of water; add few drops red food coloring with vanilla to tint frosting a delicate pink.

Lord Baltimore Filling
Makes enough to fill two 9-inch layers

½ cup flaked toasted coconut

½ cup finely chopped pecans
⅓ cup chopped candied red cherries
2 teaspoons grated orange rind
1 teaspoon almond extract
1½ cups WHITE MOUNTAIN CREAM FROSTING

1 Combine coconut, pecans, cherries, orange rind, and almond extract in a medium-size bowl.
2 Fold in WHITE MOUNTAIN CREAM FROSTING. Spread between layers of LORD BALTIMORE CAKE.

Fresh Orange Cake
Bake at 350° for 30 minutes. Makes two 9-inch layers

3 cups sifted cake flour
3 teaspoons baking powder
½ teaspoon salt
¾ cup soft shortening
1½ cups sugar
3 eggs
1 tablespoon grated orange rind
½ cup orange juice
⅔ cup milk
ORANGE BUTTER CREAM FROSTING (recipe follows)

1 Grease two 9x1½-inch layer-cake pans; dust lightly with flour; tap out any excess.
2 Sift flour, baking powder, and salt onto wax paper; reserve.
3 Combine shortening, sugar, eggs, and orange rind in large bowl of mixer; beat at high speed 3 minutes. Remove bowl from mixer.
4 Stir in flour mixture alternately with orange juice and milk, beating after each addition until batter is smooth. Pour batter into prepared pans.
5 Bake in moderate oven (350°) 30 minutes, or until centers spring back when lightly pressed with fingertip.
6 Cool layers in pans on wire racks 10 minutes; loosen around edges with a knife; turn out onto wire racks; cool completely.
7 Put layers together with part of ORANGE BUTTER CREAM FROSTING. Frost side and top with remaining frosting.

Orange Butter Cream Frosting
Makes enough to fill and frost two 9-inch layers

½ cup butter or margarine, softened
2 teaspoons grated orange rind
⅛ teaspoon salt
1 egg yolk

Fresh Orange Cake, trimmed with orange half slices.

1 package (1 pound) 10X (confectioners' powdered) sugar, sifted
¼ cup orange juice

1 Combine butter or margarine, orange rind, salt, and egg yolk in small bowl of mixer. Beat at medium speed until thoroughly blended.
2 Add sugar alternately with orange juice, beating until mixture is of good spreading consistency.

Manhattan Lemon Cake
Bake at 325° for 1 hour and 45 minutes. Makes one 10-inch tube cake

2 tablespoons very soft butter or margarine (for pan)
¼ cup fine dry bread crumbs
3¾ cups sifted cake flour
2½ teaspoons baking powder
1 teaspoon salt
1¼ cups (2½ sticks) butter or margarine (for cake)
2½ cups sugar (for cake)
5 eggs
3 tablespoons grated lemon rind
1¼ cups milk
⅔ cup sugar (for glaze)
⅓ cup lemon juice

401

1 Spread the 2 tablespoons very soft butter or margarine evenly in a 10-inch tube pan; dust evenly with dry bread crumbs. (This forms a lovely brown crust when cake is baked.)

2 Sift flour, baking powder, and salt onto wax paper; reserve.
3 Beat 1¼ cups butter or margarine, 2½ cups sugar, eggs, and lemon rind in large bowl of mixer at high speed for 3 minutes. Remove bowl from mixer.
4 Stir in flour mixture alternately with milk, beating after each addition until batter is smooth. Spoon batter carefully into prepared pan; smooth top.
5 Bake in slow oven (325°) 1¾ hours, or until top springs back when lightly pressed with fingertip.
6 Loosen cake at tube edge with a knife; turn out onto a wire rack.
7 Combine remaining ⅔ cup sugar and the lemon juice in a small saucepan. Heat slowly, stirring constantly, just until sugar is dissolved. Brush some of the glaze onto the sides of the hot cake with a soft brush, then drizzle remaining evenly over top; cool. Cut into thin wedges to serve.

Lemon Squares
Delicate lemon flavors these tiny tea treats
Bake at 350° for 45 minutes. Makes 16 two-inch squares

¾ cup sifted all-purpose flour
⅓ cup 10X (confectioners' powdered) sugar
⅓ cup ground almonds
½ cup (1 stick) butter or margarine, softened
2 eggs
1 cup sugar
1 teaspoon grated lemon rind
2 tablespoons lemon juice
½ teaspoon baking powder
¼ teaspoon salt
¾ cup flaked coconut

1 Blend flour, 10X sugar, almonds, and butter or margarine in a small bowl. Press evenly on bottom of an 8x8x2-inch baking pan.
2 Bake in moderate oven (350°) for 20 minutes.
3 Combine eggs, sugar, lemon rind and juice, baking powder, and salt in small bowl of mixer; beat at medium speed about 3 minutes, or until fluffy. Stir in coconut; pour over hot crust.
4 Bake 25 minutes longer, or until golden brown. Cool completely on a wire rack. Cut into 2-inch squares.

Fresh Apple Cake
Bake at 350° for 35 minutes. Makes three 8-inch square layers

2¾ cups sifted cake flour
1½ teaspoons apple-pie spice

1 teaspoon baking powder
1 teaspoon baking soda
1 teaspoon salt
½ cup soft shortening
1¾ cups sugar
3 eggs
2 medium-size tart cooking apples, pared, cored, and shredded (2 cups)
1 teaspoon vanilla
½ cup milk
1 cup very finely chopped walnuts
VANILLA BUTTER CREAM FROSTING (recipe follows)

1 Grease bottoms of three 8x8x2-inch cake pans; line pans with wax paper; grease paper.
2 Sift flour, apple-pie spice, baking powder, baking soda, and salt onto wax paper; reserve.
3 Beat shortening, sugar, and eggs in large bowl of mixer at high speed for 3 minutes. Remove bowl from mixer; stir in apples and vanilla.
4 Stir in flour mixture alternately with milk, beating after each addition until batter is smooth. Stir in nuts; pour batter into prepared pans.
5 Bake in moderate oven (350°) 35 minutes, or until centers spring back when they are lightly pressed with fingertip.
6 Cool layers in pans on wire racks 10 minutes; loosen around edges with a knife; turn out onto wire racks; remove wax paper; cool the layers completely.
7 Put layers together with VANILLA BUTTER CREAM FROSTING; frost sides and top with remaining frosting; garnish with walnut halves, if you wish.

Vanilla Butter Cream Frosting
Makes enough to fill and frost three 8-inch square layers

¾ cup (1½ sticks) butter or margarine
7 cups sifted 10X (confectioners' powdered) sugar (from 2 one-pound packages)
¼ cup milk
2 teaspoons vanilla
¼ teaspoon salt

Beat butter or margarine until soft in a medium-size bowl. Beat in 10X sugar, alternately with milk, vanilla, and salt until smooth and spreadable.

Holly Ribbon Cake
Bake at 350° for 25 minutes. Makes one 9-inch triple-layer cake

4 cups sifted cake flour
4 teaspoons baking powder

½ teaspoon salt
½ teaspoon ground mace
½ teaspoon ground ginger
1 cup (2 sticks) butter or margarine
2 cups sugar
4 eggs
2 teaspoons vanilla
1 cup milk
1 cup chopped pecans
½ cup candied red cherries, halved
½ cup chopped candied orange peel
½ cup golden raisins
LEMON-COCONUT FILLING (recipe follows)
1 package fluffy white frosting mix

1 Grease three 9x1½-inch layer-cake pans; flour lightly, tapping out any excess.
2 Sift flour, baking powder, salt, mace, and ginger onto wax paper.
3 Cream butter or margarine with sugar until fluffy-light in a large bowl; beat in eggs, one at a time, and vanilla.
4 Beat in flour mixture, alternately with milk, until well-blended.
5 Measure 2 cups of the batter into a medium-size bowl; stir in pecans, cherries, orange peel, and raisins. Pour into one of the prepared pans; pour plain batter into two remaining pans, dividing evenly.
6 Bake in moderate oven (350°) 25 minutes, or until tops spring back when lightly pressed with fingertip. (Fruit layer may need an additional 5 minutes' baking time.)
7 Cool in pans 10 minutes on wire racks. Loosen around edges with a knife; turn out onto racks; cool completely.
8 While layers cool, make LEMON-COCONUT FILLING; cool.
9 Spread LEMON-COCONUT FILLING over fruit layer and one of the plain layers. Stack layers on a serving plate, placing fruit layer in middle.
10 Prepare fluffy white frosting mix with boiling water, following label directions. Spread over side and top of cake. Trim with candied red cherries and leaves cut from angelica to resemble holly, if you wish.

LEMON-COCONUT FILLING—Mix ⅓ cup sugar and 2 tablespoons cornstarch in a medium-size saucepan; stir in ¾ cup water. Cook, stirring constantly, until mixture thickens and boils 3 minutes. Beat 1 egg yolk slightly in a small bowl; slowly beat in about half of the hot mixture, then stir back into saucepan. Cook, stirring constantly, 1 minute longer; remove from heat. Stir in 1 tablespoon butter or margarine, 1 teaspoon grated lemon rind, 3 tablespoons lemon juice, and ½ cup cookie coconut. Cool. Makes about 1½ cups.

Holly Ribbon Cake decked with cherries and angelica.

Candy-Cake Castle
Little architects will be delighted to help build this charmer. It's big, but any left will freeze perfectly.
Bake at 350° for 45 minutes. Makes 16 to 20 servings

403

2 recipes PARTY CAKE (recipe follows
  CASTLE CAKE FROSTING (recipe follows)
4 sugar ice-cream cones
2 packages (3 ounces each) yellow pillow-shape mint-flavor candies
2 packages (3 ounces each) pink pillow-shape mint-flavor candies
1 package (3 ounces) white pillow-shape mint-flavor candies
2 pints vanilla ice cream
2 pints strawberry ice cream

CAKE BAKER'S ART

1 Save up your empty condensed-soup cans (the about-10-ounce size) for you will need eight for baking cylinder cakes to make the castle "turrets," along with one large shallow baking pan to make the cake for castle "walls." Brush eight dry, clean condensed-soup cans and one baking pan, 13x9x2, well with vegetable oil; line bottoms of each with wax paper; grease paper.

2 Make cake batter for soup cans: Prepare first recipe of PARTY CAKE. Spoon ¾ cup batter into each can; set, not touching, in large shallow pan for easy handling.

3 Bake in moderate oven (350°) 45 minutes, or until a long thin metal skewer inserted in cakes comes out clean.

4 While small cakes bake, prepare second recipe of PARTY CAKE; pour batter into prepared baking pan.

5 Bake in moderate oven (350°) 45 minutes, or until top springs back when lightly pressed with fingertip.

6 Cool cakes in cans and pan on wire racks 5 minutes; loosen around edges with knife; turn out onto racks; peel off paper; cool completely.

7 While cakes cool, make CASTLE CAKE FROSTING.

8 Make castle: Cover a piece of heavy cardboard, 15x12, with foil for floor of castle.

9 Spread a thin coating of yellow frosting over ice cream cones, then press candies, alternating colors, in rows into frosting to cover cones completely. (Set cones and remaining candies aside for Step 13.)

10 Cut flat cake in half lengthwise, then cut a 4½-inch-long piece from one end of each to make two large and two small pieces. Stand the two large pieces, long cut sides down, about 8 inches apart on foil floor. Stand the two small pieces, cut sides down, just inside the large ones to form four walls.

11 Set one cylinder cake at each corner to form lower part of each turret; cover tops with a little frosting, then stand another cylinder cake on top of each. (To keep straight, hold in place with long thin metal skewers.) Frost all over with a thin coating of yellow frosting; let dry. (This forms a thin film for final frosting.)

12 Frost castle all over with remaining yellow frosting, smoothing on a little extra as needed to cover lines where cake pieces meet.

13 Fill a cake-decorating set with pink frosting and, using writing tip, outline "stones" and

The birthday child will flip over this fairytale ice cream-and-cake castle turreted with pastel peppermints.

"doors". Stand ice cream cones on cylinder cakes to make tops of turrets; insert a paper flag in each, if you wish. Press remaining pink candies around base of turrets and tops of walls.

14 Scoop ice cream into balls; place on cookie sheet; freeze until firm. Fit a piece of foil into castle "courtyard" to form a bowl for ice cream.

15 When ready to serve, fill foil bowl with ice cream balls. To serve cake, cut side walls first, then front and back. Lift cones off turrets, then remove skewers and slice cylinder cakes.

Party Cake

Just right for a birthday castle—equally good as a family treat. Its secret ingredient—fruity gelatin—gives it a candylike flavor.

Bake at 350° for 45 minutes. Makes 1 cake, 13x9x2, or 8 small cylinder cakes

    3 cups sifted cake flour
    4 teaspoons baking powder
    1 teaspoon salt
    ¾ cup vegetable shortening
    1 cup sugar
    1 package (3 ounces) fruit-flavor gelatin (your favorite flavor)
    3 eggs
    1 teaspoon vanilla
    1 teaspoon lemon extract
    1¼ cups milk

1 Prepare baking pan, 13x9x2, or eight condensed-soup cans, as in Step 1 of CANDY-CAKE CASTLE *(recipe precedes)*.

2 Sift cake flour, baking powder, and salt onto wax paper.

3 Cream shortening with sugar and dry fruit-flavor gelatin until fluffy in large bowl with spoon or electric mixer at medium speed. Add eggs, one at a time, beating well after each; beat in vanilla and lemon extract.

4 Add sifted dry ingredients, a third at a time, alternately with milk, stirring with a spoon or beating with mixer at low speed, just until blended. Pour into prepared pan or soup cans.

5 Bake in moderate oven (350°) 45 minutes, or until top of cake in pan springs back when lightly pressed with fingertip, or until a long thin metal skewer inserted in cylinder cakes comes out clean.

6 Cool in pan or cans on wire rack 5 minutes; loosen around edges with knife; turn out onto wire rack; peel off wax paper; cool all cakes completely before decorating for castle.

Castle Cake Frosting
Makes enough to frost one castle cake

    1 cup (2 sticks) butter or margarine
    2 packages (1 pound each) 10X (confectioners' powdered) sugar, sifted
    ¼ cup light corn syrup
    3 tablespoons milk
    2 teaspoons vanilla
    ¼ teaspoon salt
      Red food coloring
      Yellow food coloring

1 Cream butter or margarine until soft in large bowl. Beat in 10X sugar, alternately with corn syrup and milk, then beat in vanilla and salt. Continue beating until frosting is thick and creamy-smooth.

2 Spoon about 1 cupful into a small bowl; blend in a few drops red food coloring to tint a delicate pink. Tint remaining yellow with yellow food coloring.

Cherry-Almond Sweetheart Cake
Any young lady would be tickled pink over this tribute to her birthday.
Bake at 350° for 35 minutes. Makes one heart-shape or one 9-inch double-layer cake

    2¼ cups sifted cake flour
    1½ cups sugar
    3 teaspoons baking powder
    1 teaspoon salt
    2 eggs, separated
    ⅓ cup vegetable oil
    1 cup milk
    1 teaspoon vanilla
    1 teaspoon almond extract
      ROYAL CHERRY FILLING (recipe follows)
      WHITE CLOUD FROSTING (recipe follows)

1 Grease bottoms of two heart-shape layer-cake pans or two 9x1½-inch layer-cake pans; line with wax paper; grease paper.

2 Sift cake flour, 1 cup sugar, baking powder, and salt into large bowl.

3 Beat egg whites until foamy-white and double in volume in medium-size bowl; sprinkle in remaining ½ cup sugar *very slowly*, 1 tablespoon

405

at a time, beating all the time until meringue forms soft peaks.

4 Blend vegetable oil and ½ cup milk into flour mixture, then beat 2 minutes with mixer at medium speed or beat vigorously by hand for 150 strokes. Stir in egg yolks, remaining ½ cup milk, vanilla, and almond extract; beat 1 minute at medium speed, or 100 strokes.

5 Fold in meringue until no streaks of white remain. Pour into prepared pans, dividing evenly.

6 Bake in moderate oven (350°) 35 minutes, or until tops spring back when lightly pressed with fingertip.

7 Cool in pans on wire racks 5 minutes; loosen around edges with knife; turn out onto racks; peel off paper; cool completely.

8 Make ROYAL CHERRY FILLING. Split each cake layer in half crosswise; put together with ROYAL CHERRY FILLING between each; place on serving plate.

9 Make WHITE CLOUD FROSTING. Frost top and side of cake, making deep swirls with tip of spoon. Decorate with birthday-cake candles. (If cake is baked in round layer-cake pans, outline a heart shape with candles on top of cake.)

Royal Cherry Filling

Colorful with bits of cherries and crunchy with slivers of almonds.
Makes enough to fill one heart-shape or one 9-inch double-layer cake

  ½ *cup sugar*
  4 *tablespoons all-purpose flour*
  ¼ *teaspoon salt*
  2 *egg yolks*
1½ *cups milk, scalded*
  ¼ *cup chopped drained maraschino cherries*
  ¼ *cup chopped toasted slivered almonds
      (from a 5-ounce can)*
  2 *tablespoons butter or margarine*
  1 *teaspoon vanilla*
  1 *teaspoon almond extract*

1 Combine sugar, flour, and salt in 1-cup measure. Beat egg yolks slightly with fork in small bowl; stir in about ½ cup scalded milk, then slowly stir back into remaining scalded milk in saucepan; stir in dry ingredients.

2 Cook, stirring constantly, over medium heat, until mixture thickens and boils 1 minute; remove from heat.

3 Stir in remaining ingredients; cool completely before filling cake.

White Cloud Frosting

Perfect for a special-occasion cake—and simple to make
Makes enough to frost one heart-shape or one 9-inch double-layer cake

1½ *cups sugar*
  ¼ *cup water*
  2 *unbeaten egg whites*
  2 *tablespoons light corn syrup*
  ¼ *teaspoon salt*
  1 *teaspoon vanilla*

1 Combine all ingredients in top of double boiler; beat until blended.

2 Place over simmering water; cook, beating constantly with an electric or rotary beater, 5 minutes, or until mixture triples in volume and holds firm marks of beater; remove from heat.

3 Spread on cake at once, while frosting is fluffy-light.

Queen's Coconut Cake

This triple-layer beauty boasts a tart lemony filling and snowy coconut frosting
Bake at 350° for 30 minutes. Makes one 9-inch triple-layer cake

  3 *cups sifted cake flour*
  4 *teaspoons baking powder*
  1 *teaspoon salt*
  ¾ *cup vegetable shortening*
1¾ *cups sugar*
  3 *eggs*
  1 *teaspoon vanilla*
  ½ *teaspoon lemon extract*
1¼ *cups milk*
      LEMON-BUTTERCUP FILLING (recipe follows)
      FLUFFY FROSTING (recipe follows)
  1 *can (3½ ounces) flaked coconut*
      Sugar-candy flowers

1 Grease bottoms of three 9x1½-inch layer-cake pans; line pans with wax paper; grease paper.

2 Sift cake flour, baking powder, and salt onto wax paper.

3 Cream shortening with sugar until fluffy in large bowl with spoon or electric mixer at medium speed. Beat in eggs, one at a time, beating well after each; beat in vanilla and lemon extract.

4 Add sifted dry ingredients, a third at a time, alternately with milk, stirring with a spoon or beating with mixer at low speed, just until blended. Pour into prepared pans.

5 Bake in moderate oven (350°) 30 minutes, or until centers spring back when lightly touched with fingertip.

Queen's Coconut Cake with a lemon-flavored filling and a cloud-light white frosting drifted with coconut. To trim: delicate sugar-candy flowers.

6 Cool in pans on wire racks 5 minutes; loosen around edges with knife; turn out onto racks; peel off wax paper; cool completely.
7 Put layers together with LEMON-BUTTERCUP FILLING; frost top and side with FLUFFY FROSTING. Sprinkle coconut around side and over top; arrange sugar-candy flowers to form a bouquet on top.

Lemon-Buttercup Filling
Makes enough to fill one 9-inch triple-layer cake

½ cup sugar
3 tablespoons cornstarch
¼ teaspoon salt
2 egg yolks
¾ cup water
⅓ cup lemon juice
2 tablespoons butter or margarine

1 Mix sugar, cornstarch, and salt in medium-size saucepan; stir in egg yolks and water.
2 Cook, stirring constantly, until mixture thickens and boils 3 minutes; remove from heat. Stir in lemon juice and butter or margarine until well-blended; cool completely.

Fluffy Frosting
Makes enough to frost top and side of one 9-inch triple-layer cake

2 egg whites
¼ teaspoon cream of tartar
2 tablespoons light corn syrup
2½ tablespoons water
1½ teaspoons vanilla
½ teaspoon lemon extract
1 pound 10X (confectioners' powdered) sugar, sifted

1 Combine egg whites and cream of tartar in medium-size bowl; beat until egg whites stand in firm peaks.
2 Combine light corn syrup, water, vanilla, and lemon extract in a cup. Add alternately with 10X sugar to egg-white mixture, beating well after each addition, until frosting is creamy-stiff and easy to spread.

Viennese Ribbons
Bake at 350° for 10 minutes. Makes 3 dozen

2¼ cups sifted all-purpose flour
¼ teaspoon salt
1 cup (2 sticks) butter or margarine
1 cup sugar
3 eggs
1 teaspoon vanilla
1 can (5 ounces) toasted slivered almonds (1 cup)
1 cup (8-ounce carton) dairy sour cream
9 tablespoons red raspberry jam (from a 12-ounce jar)
9 tablespoons apricot jam (from a 12-ounce jar)
BUTTER-RICH FROSTING (recipe follows)
Red food coloring

1 Grease backs of two baking pans, 9x9x2, well; dust lightly with flour, then tap off.
2 Sift flour and salt onto wax paper or foil.
3 Cream butter or margarine in a large bowl with spoon or electric mixer at medium speed; add sugar gradually, beating until fluffy.
4 Beat in eggs, one at a time, until fluffy; beat in vanilla.
5 Add sifted dry ingredients, a third at a time, stirring with a spoon or beating with mixer at low speed just until blended.
6 Spread ½ cup of the batter on each prepared pan to within ¼ inch of edges to make a thin layer.
7 Bake in moderate oven (350°) 10 minutes, or just until golden around edges. Carefully

408

loosen layers with a spatula; remove and cool on wire racks. Repeat Steps 6 and 7, washing, greasing, and flouring pans before each baking, to make seven layers in all.
8 Put almonds through a food chopper, using fine blade, or chop very fine; stir into sour cream in a small bowl.
9 Put cakes together this way: Place one layer on a cutting board or cookie sheet; spread with 3 tablespoons of the raspberry jam, then with ¼ cup of the sour-cream mixture. Place second layer on top; spread with 3 tablespoons of the apricot jam and ¼ cup of the sour-cream mixture. Repeat with 4 more layers, alternating jam fillings each time; cover with remaining layer. Place one of the square baking pans on top, weighing it down with an unopened about 2-pound food can, to press layers together. Chill overnight.
10 Make BUTTER-RICH FROSTING. Measure 3 tablespoons into a cup; tint pink with a drop or two of red food coloring.
11 Trim edges of chilled cake even with a sharp knife; spread top with white frosting. While white is still soft, drizzle pink frosting from tip of knife in thin straight lines, ½ inch apart, over white, then draw knife through frosting and across lines every ½ inch to make a pretty pattern. Chill until frosting is firm.
12 Cut cake into 6 strips about 1½ inches wide with a very sharp knife, then cut each strip into 6 pieces. (Wrap any leftover cakes in transparent wrap and store in the refrigerator.)

BUTTER-RICH FROSTING—Combine 1½ cups sifted 10X (confectioners' powdered) sugar, dash of salt, 3 tablespoons butter or margarine, 2 tablespoons milk, and 1 teaspoon vanilla in a medium-size bowl; beat until creamy-smooth. Makes about ½ cup.

Strawberry Ribbon Cake Desserts
It's perfect for your best valentine or a birthday celebration any time
Bake at 375° for 35 minutes. Makes one 8-inch four-layer cake

3 cups sifted cake flour
2½ teaspoons baking powder
½ teaspoon salt
1 cup (2 sticks) butter or margarine
2 cups sugar
4 eggs
1 teaspoon vanilla

Two spring beauties: Almond Meringue Torte (background) and four-layer, pink and yellow Strawberry Ribbon Cake with baked-on meringue icing.

½ teaspoon almond extract
¾ cup milk
⅛ teaspoon red food coloring
   STRAWBERRY BUTTER CREAM (recipe follows)

1 Grease two baking pans, 8x8x2; dust with flour.
2 Sift cake flour, baking powder, and salt onto wax paper.
3 Cream butter or margarine until soft in a large bowl; beat in sugar gradually until fluffy. Beat in eggs, one at a time, until fluffy again, then flavorings.
4 Stir in flour mixture, alternately with milk, just until blended. Spoon half the batter into one pan; stir food coloring into remaining batter; pour into second pan.
5 Bake in moderate oven (375°) 35 minutes, or until centers spring back when pressed with fingertip. Cool layers in pans on wire racks 10 minutes; turn out onto racks; cool completely.
6 Split each cooled layer; put together, alternating pink and yellow, with part of the STRAWBERRY BUTTER CREAM; frost sides and top with remaining.

Strawberry Butter Cream

1 package (3 or 4 ounces) cream cheese
4 tablespoons (½ stick) butter or margarine
⅓ cup mashed fresh strawberries
1 package (1 pound) 10X (confectioners' powdered) sugar

1 Blend cream cheese with butter or margarine until fluffy in a medium-size bowl; beat in strawberries.
2 Stir in 2 cups of the 10X sugar until smooth.
3 Measure out 1½ cups of the mixture for filling.
4 Beat remaining 10X sugar into remaining mixture in bowl for frosting.

409

Almond Meringue Torte
Layers of meringue-topped cake, cream, and almonds make this memorable treat
Bake at 350° for 30 minutes. Makes one 8-inch double-layer torte

1¼ cups sifted cake flour
1 teaspoon baking powder

¼ teaspoon salt
½ cup (1 stick) butter or margarine
1¼ cups sugar
4 eggs, separated
1 teaspoon vanilla
¼ cup milk
½ cup toasted slivered almonds (from a 5-ounce can)
1 cup cream for whipping
1 tablespoon 10X (confectioners' powdered) sugar
½ teaspoon cinnamon

1 Butter bottoms of two 8x1½-inch layer-cake pans; dust with flour.
2 Sift cake flour, baking powder, and salt onto wax paper.
3 Cream butter or margarine until soft in a medium-size bowl; beat in ½ cup of the sugar gradually until fluffy. Beat in egg yolks, one at a time, until blended, then vanilla. Stir in flour mixture, alternately with milk, just until blended; spoon into prepared pans.
4 Beat egg whites until foamy-white in a large bowl; beat in remaining ¾ cup sugar, 1 tablespoon at a time, until meringue stands in firm peaks. Spread ⅓ over batter in each pan. Press remaining meringue through a pastry bag, or use a teaspoon, to make rosettes around edge and in center of one layer. Sprinkle both layers with almonds.
5 Bake in moderate oven (350°) 30 minutes, or until meringue is delicately browned.
6 Cool layers in pans on wire racks 5 minutes; loosen around edges with a knife; turn each out onto palm of hand, then place, meringue side up, on racks; cool completely.
7 Beat cream with 10X sugar and cinnamon until stiff in a medium-size bowl.
8 Place plain meringue layer on a serving plate; spread with cream mixture; top with fancy layer. Chill until serving time.

410

Praline Applesauce Cake
For easy no-fuss toting, the spicy-rich cake is crowned with a broiled-on brown-sugar-pecan topping
Bake at 350° for 35 minutes. Makes one cake 13x9x2

2¾ cups sifted cake flour
1⅓ cups sugar
1½ teaspoons baking soda
¼ teaspoon baking powder
1½ teaspoons ground cinnamon
½ teaspoon ground cloves

½ teaspoon salt
½ cup soft vegetable shortening
1 can or jar (about 1 pound) applesauce (1¾ cups)
2 eggs
1½ cups seedless raisins
PRALINE TOPPING (recipe follows)

1 Grease a baking pan, 13x9x2; dust lightly with flour, tapping out any excess.
2 Sift cake flour, sugar, soda, baking powder, cinnamon, cloves, and salt into a large bowl.
3 Add shortening and applesauce; beat, scraping down side of bowl often, 2 minutes at medium speed with an electric beater.
4 Add eggs; beat 2 minutes longer, or until blended; fold in raisins. Pour into prepared pan.
5 Bake in moderate oven (350°) 35 minutes, or until center springs back when lightly pressed with fingertip. Remove from oven; cool in pan on a wire rack 15 minutes. Raise oven temperature to BROIL.
6 Make PRALINE TOPPING; spread evenly over warm cake.
7 Broil, 6 inches from heat, 3 to 4 minutes, or until topping bubbles up and turns golden. Cool on a wire rack. Cut into squares.
PRALINE TOPPING—Cream ½ cup (1 stick) butter or margarine with ¾ cup firmly packed brown sugar until fluffy-light in a medium-size bowl; beat in ¼ cup cream until smooth, then stir in 1½ cups chopped pecans and ⅔ cup flaked coconut.
NOTE: To decorate cake, lay several inch-wide strips of wax paper diagonally across top; hold in place with wooden picks. Sieve 10X (confectioners' powdered) sugar generously over cake, then carefully lift off paper strips.

Double-Date Cake
Bake at 350° for 1 hour. Makes one 8-inch square cake

1 package (8 ounces) pitted dates
1 cup boiling water
½ cup (1 stick) butter or margarine
1 cup sugar
1 teaspoon vanilla
1 egg, beaten
1⅓ cups sifted all-purpose flour
1 teaspoon baking soda
¼ teaspoon salt
½ cup chopped pecans
DATE FROSTING (recipe follows)

1 Chop dates; combine with boiling water, butter or margarine, sugar, and vanilla in a medium-size heavy saucepan. Cook, stirring constantly, 10 minutes, or until mixture is slightly thick. Remove from heat; cool. Stir in beaten egg.

2 Sift flour, soda, and salt into date mixture, a little at a time, blending well; stir in pecans. Pour into a greased and wax-paper-lined pan, 8x8x2.

3 Bake in moderate oven (350°) 1 hour, or until center springs back when lightly pressed with fingertip. Remove from oven; spread DATE FROSTING on top.

4 Cut into small squares. Serve warm or cold with whipped cream, if you wish.

DATE FROSTING—Chop 1 package (8 ounces) pitted dates; combine with 1 cup boiling water, ½ cup (1 stick) butter or margarine, and 1 cup sugar in a medium-size heavy saucepan. Cook, stirring constantly, about 20 minutes, or until mixture is very thick. Remove from heat and stir in ½ cup chopped pecans. Cool to luke-warm. Makes enough to frost the top of 1 eight-inch square cake.

Banana-Nut Cake
Bake at 350° for 30 minutes. Makes two 9-inch layers

2⅓ cups sifted cake flour
2½ teaspoons baking powder
½ teaspoon baking soda
½ teaspoon salt
½ teaspoon ground cinnamon
 1 cup mashed ripe bananas (2 medium-size)
½ cup buttermilk
½ cup (1 stick) butter or margarine
1¼ cups sugar
 2 eggs
¼ teaspoon vanilla
¾ cup chopped walnuts
 RUM BUTTER CREAM FROSTING (recipe follows)

1 Grease two 9x1½-inch layer-cake pans; dust lightly with flour; tap out any excess.

2 Sift flour, baking powder, baking soda, salt, and cinnamon onto wax paper; reserve. Stir buttermilk into mashed bananas in a small bowl; reserve.

3 Beat butter or margarine, sugar, and eggs in large bowl of mixer at high speed 3 minutes. Remove bowl from mixer.

4 Stir in flour mixture alternately with banana-milk mixture, beating after each addition until batter is smooth. Stir in vanilla and ¼ cup chopped nuts; pour batter into prepared pans.

5 Bake in moderate oven (350°) 30 minutes,

or until centers spring back when lightly pressed with fingertip.

6 Cool layers in pans on wire racks 10 minutes; loosen around edges with a knife; turn out onto wire racks; cool completely.

7 Put layers together with RUM BUTTER CREAM FROSTING; frost side and top with remaining frosting. Press remaining ½ cup chopped nuts on sides of cake. Dip banana slices in orange or pineapple juice to keep white; garnish top of cake, if you wish.

Rum Butter Cream Frosting
Makes enough to fill and frost two 9-inch layers

⅓ cup butter or margarine
3½ cups sifted 10X (confectioners' powdered) sugar
¼ cup milk
1½ teaspoons rum extract

1 Beat butter or margarine in a medium-size bowl until soft.

2 Add 10X sugar alternately with rum extract and milk until creamy-smooth.

Old-Time Nut Cake
Bake at 350° for 1 hour and 5 minutes. Makes one 9-inch tube cake

2¾ cups sifted cake flour
 2 teaspoons baking powder
 1 teaspoon salt
 1 cup (2 sticks) butter or margarine
1¾ cups sugar
 4 eggs
⅔ cup milk
 2 teaspoons vanilla
 1 cup very finely chopped nuts (use hickory nuts, black walnuts, or pecans)
 BROWN-BUTTER ICING (recipe follows)

1 Grease a 9-inch tube pan or Bundt pan; dust lightly with flour; tap out any excess.

2 Sift flour, baking powder, and salt onto wax paper; reserve.

3 Beat butter or margarine, sugar, and eggs in large bowl of mixer at high speed 3 minutes. Remove bowl from mixer.

4 Stir in dry ingredients alternately with milk, beating after each addition until batter is smooth.

5 Stir in vanilla and nuts. Pour batter into prepared pan.

6 Bake in moderate oven (350°) 1 hour and 5 minutes, or until center springs back when lightly pressed with fingertip.

7 Cool in pan on wire rack 10 minutes; loosen

cake around tube and outside with a knife; turn out onto wire rack; cool completely.

8 Frost top and side with BROWN-BUTTER ICING.

Brown Butter Icing
Makes enough to frost one 9-inch tube cake

½ cup (1 stick) butter or margarine
1 package (1 pound) 10X (confectioners' powdered) sugar, sifted
¼ cup milk

1 Heat butter or margarine slowly in a medium-size saucepan until liquid bubbles up, is very foamy, then settles and is lightly browned. *Remove from heat at once.* (Watch carefully to prevent over-browning; browning takes only 3 to 5 minutes.)

2 Pour browned butter over 10X sugar in large bowl; mix until evenly crumbly.

3 Drizzle milk over; blend until smooth. Add 1 to 2 teaspoonfuls more milk, if necessary to make smooth and spreadable.

Coffee Walnut Torte
Bake at 350° for 30 minutes. Makes one 9-inch, 4-layer torte

2½ cups sifted cake flour
1⅔ cups sugar
3 teaspoons baking powder
1 teaspoon salt
⅔ cup soft vegetable shortening
1¼ cups milk
6 egg yolks
2 teaspoons vanilla

Coffee Walnut Torte crowned with crunchy nut brittle.

412

¾ cup apricot preserves
COFFEE FROSTING (recipe follows)
WALNUT BRITTLE (recipe follows)

1 Grease two 9x1½-inch round layer-cake pans; dust lightly with flour; tap out any excess.

2 Sift flour, sugar, baking powder, and salt into large bowl of electric mixer. Add shortening and 1 cup of the milk. Beat at medium speed 2 minutes. Add remaining ¼ cup milk, egg yolks, and vanilla. Beat at medium speed 2 minutes longer. Pour into prepared pans, spreading evenly.

3 Bake in moderate oven (350°) 30 minutes, or until centers spring back when lightly pressed with fingertip. Cool in pans on wire racks 10 minutes. Loosen layers around edges with a knife; turn out onto racks; cool completely. Split each layer, using a sawing motion with a sharp knife.

4 Place one split cake layer on serving plate. Spread with ¼ cup of the apricot preserves and ½ of the COFFEE FROSTING; repeat with 2 more layers, spreading with preserves and frosting, ending with a plain layer on top. Frost top layer, reserving part of the COFFEE FROSTING for garnish. Sprinkle WALNUT BRITTLE over top of cake. Fit a pastry bag with a small star tip; fill bag with remaining frosting and garnish cake in middle and around edge with rosettes.

Coffee Frosting
Makes enough frosting for one 4-layer torte

½ cup (1 stick) butter or margarine, softened
1 package 10X (confectioners' powdered) sugar, sifted
1 tablespoon instant coffee powder
3 tablespoons coffee liqueur
2 tablespoons milk

Cream butter or margarine and part of the sugar. Combine coffee, coffee liqueur, and milk in a cup. Add alternately with remaining sugar to creamed mixture, beating until smooth.

Walnut Brittle
Spread ¾ cup granulated sugar in a small heavy skillet; heat slowly until sugar melts and starts to turn pale golden in color. Stir in ½ cup chopped walnuts and immediately pour out onto a cooky sheet, spreading evenly. Cool completely. Break into small pieces. Makes about 1 cup.

Poppy Seed Cake
Bake at 350° for 30 minutes. Makes two 9-inch square layers

The basics of a satin-smooth "butter" cream frosting, equally good, by the way, made with soft margarine.

1 cup poppy seeds
1½ cups milk
3 cups sifted cake flour
3 teaspoons baking powder
1 teaspoon salt
4 egg whites
¾ cup (1½ sticks) butter or margarine
1½ cups sugar
1 teaspoon vanilla
  LEMON BUTTER CREAM FROSTING (recipe follows)

1 Grease two 9x9x2-inch cake pans; dust lightly with flour; tap out any excess.
2 Combine poppy seeds and ¾ cup of the milk in a small saucepan. Heat to boiling. Remove from heat; cover saucepan. Allow to stand until milk is absorbed, about 1 hour.
3 Sift flour, baking powder, and salt onto wax paper; reserve.
4 Beat egg whites until foamy-white and double in volume in a medium-size bowl; beat in ½ cup of the sugar, 1 tablespoon at a time, until meringue forms soft peaks; reserve.

5 Beat butter or margarine and remaining 1 cup sugar in large bowl of mixer at high speed for 3 minutes; blend in poppy seed mixture.
6 Stir in flour mixture alternately with the remaining ¾ cup milk and vanilla, beating after each addition until batter is smooth.
7 Fold meringue into batter until no streaks of white remain; pour into prepared pans.
8 Bake in moderate oven (350°) 30 minutes, or until centers spring back when lightly pressed with fingertip.
9 Cool layers in pans on wire racks 10 minutes; loosen around edges with a knife; turn out onto wire racks; cool completely.
10 Put layers together with LEMON BUTTER CREAM FROSTING; frost sides and top with remaining frosting.

413

Lemon Butter Cream Frosting
Makes enough to fill and frost two 9-inch square layers

½ cup (1 stick) butter or margarine

1 package (1 pound) 10X (confectioners' powdered) sugar, sifted
½ teaspoon grated lemon rind
   Dash of salt
3 tablespoons lemon juice
1 tablespoon milk

Beat butter or margarine until soft in a medium-size bowl. Beat in 10X sugar alternately
with lemon rind, salt, lemon juice, and milk.
Continue beating until smooth and spreadable.

●

Ribbon Spice Cake
Bake at 350° for 35 minutes. Makes three 9-inch
layers

3½ cups sifted cake flour
3 teaspoons baking powder
1 teaspoon salt
1 cup (2 sticks) butter or margarine, softened
2½ cups sugar
4 eggs
1 cup milk
1 teaspoon vanilla
3 tablespoons molasses
1 teaspoon pumpkin-pie spice
   BROWN SUGAR FLUFFY FROSTING (recipe
   follows)

1 Grease three 9x1½-inch layer-cake pans; dust
lightly with flour; tap out any excess.
2 Sift flour, baking powder, and salt onto wax
paper; reserve.
3 Beat butter, sugar, and eggs in large bowl
of mixer at high speed 3 minutes.
4 Stir in flour mixture alternately with milk and
vanilla, beating after each addition until batter
is smooth.
5 Pour ⅓ of batter into each of 2 prepared pans.
Stir molasses and pumpkin-pie spice into remaining batter; pour into third prepared pan.
6 Bake in moderate oven (350°) 35 minutes,
or until centers spring back when lightly pressed
in center with fingertip.
7 Cool layers in pans on wire racks 10 minutes;
loosen around edges with a knife; turn out onto
wire racks; cool completely.
8 Put layers together with BROWN SUGAR FLUFFY
FROSTING; frost side and top with remaining
frosting.

●

Brown Sugar Fluffy Frosting
Makes enough to fill and frost one 9-inch triple
layer cake

1 package (1 pound) light brown sugar
3 egg whites

¼ cup boiling water
1 tablespoon light corn syrup
¼ teaspoon cream of tartar
   Dash of salt
   Dash of ground mace

1 Combine all ingredients in the top of a double
boiler; beat until well-blended.
2 Place over simmering water; cook, beating
constantly with an electric mixer at high speed,
10 minutes, or until mixture triples in volume
and holds firm marks of beaters; remove from
heat.
3 Frost cake at once.

●

Spice Cupcakes
Tender little spicecakes crowned with fluffy
meringue
Bake at 350° for 30 minutes. Makes 12 cupcakes

1½ cups sifted cake flour
½ teaspoon baking soda
1¼ teaspoons pumpkin-pie spice
1 cup firmly packed brown sugar
½ cup (1 stick) butter or margarine, softened
⅔ cup milk
2 eggs, separated
½ teaspoon vanilla
¼ teaspoon cream of tartar
¼ cup granulated sugar
¼ cup ground pecans

1 Sift flour, baking soda, and pumpkin-pie spice
into large bowl of mixer; stir in brown sugar.
Add butter or margarine and milk; beat at low
speed 1½ minutes. Add egg yolks and vanilla;
beat 1½ minutes longer. Fill 12 greased muffin-
pan cups half full with batter.
2 Bake in moderate oven (350°) for 30 minutes.
3 Beat egg whites and cream of tartar until
foamy-white in small bowl of mixer. Beat in
granulated sugar until meringue stands in firm
peaks. Fold in nuts; spread on cupcakes.
4 Broil, 6 inches from heat, 4 minutes, or until
golden.

●

Our Best Gingerbread
Bake at 350° for 30 minutes. Makes one cake,
13x9x2

2½ cups sifted all-purpose flour
1½ teaspoons baking soda
1 teaspoon ground ginger
1 teaspoon ground cinnamon
½ teaspoon salt
½ cup soft vegetable shortening
½ cup sugar

1 cup molasses
1 egg
1 cup hot water

1 Sift flour, soda, ginger, cinnamon, and salt onto wax paper.
2 Cream shortening with sugar until fluffy in a large bowl; beat in molasses and egg.
3 Stir in flour mixture, half at a time, just until blended; beat in hot water until smooth. Pour into a well-greased baking pan, 13x9x2.
4 Bake in moderate oven (350°) 30 minutes, or until center springs back when lightly pressed with fingertip.
5 Leave in pan to cool on a wire rack, or let cool 10 minutes, then loosen around edge with a knife and turn out onto rack. Cut into big squares; serve warm or cold, plain or with a topper of your choice.

Lemon Gingerbread
Fresh lemon slices baked with your own gingerbread add a sparkly touch to this old favorite
Bake at 350° for 40 minutes. Makes 10 servings

3 tablespoons butter or margarine, softened
¼ cup sugar
1 lemon, sliced thinly
1⅔ cups sifted all-purpose flour
1 teaspoon baking soda

1 teaspoon ground cinnamon
¾ teaspoon ground ginger
½ teaspoon salt
⅓ cup vegetable shortening
⅓ cup sugar (for batter)
⅔ cup dark molasses
1 egg
½ cup hot water

1 Butter a 9-inch (8 cup) ring mold generously with butter or margarine, making sure there is a thick layer on bottom of ring mold. Sprinkle the ¼ cup sugar evenly onto the bottom of ring (do not coat sides with sugar); arrange lemon slices, overlapping slightly, in a layer over sugar.
2 Sift flour, baking soda, cinnamon, ginger and salt onto wax paper.
3 Beat shortening and the ⅓ cup sugar until fluffy and light in a large bowl; beat in molasses and egg. Stir in flour mixture, half at a time, blending well after each addition. Stir in hot water. Carefully pour batter over lemon slices in prepared pan.
4 Bake in moderate oven (350°) 40 minutes, or until center springs back when lightly pressed with fingertip.
5 Loosen cake around edge and center with a sharp knife; immediately invert onto serving plate; let stand 5 minutes; lift off pan.

Luscious Devil's Food Cake
Bake at 350° for 30 minutes. Makes two 9-inch layers

Gingerbread, rich and dark, baked in a ring mold lined with overlapping thinnest slices of lemon.

415

4 squares unsweetened chocolate
1½ cups sugar
1½ cups milk
1 teaspoon white vinegar
2 cups sifted cake flour
3 teaspoons baking powder
½ teaspoon baking soda
½ teaspoon salt
2 eggs, separated
½ cup (1 stick) butter or margarine
1 teaspoon vanilla
CREAM VELVET FROSTING (recipe follows)

1 Grease two 9x1½-inch layer-cake pans; dust lightly with flour; tap out any excess

2 Combine chocolate, ½ cup of the sugar, and 1 cup of the milk in a small heavy saucepan. Cook, stirring constantly, until mixture thickens and turns a deep chocolate color. Cool slightly.

3 Stir white vinegar into the remaining ½ cup milk in a cup to sour; reserve.

4 Sift flour, baking powder, baking soda, and salt onto wax paper; reserve.

5 Beat butter or margarine, remaining 1 cup sugar and egg yolks in large bowl of mixer at high speed 3 minutes. Beat in cooled chocolate mixture until light and fluffy at medium speed on mixer.

6 Stir in flour mixture alternately with soured milk and vanilla, beating after each addition until batter is smooth.

7 Beat egg whites until stiff but not dry in a small bowl; fold into batter; pour batter into prepared pans.

8 Bake in moderate oven (350°) 30 minutes, or until centers spring back when lightly pressed with fingertip.

9 Cool layers in pans on wire racks 10 minutes; loosen around edges with a knife; turn out onto wire racks; cool completely.

10 Put layers together with CHOCOLATE VELVET FROSTING; frost side and top with remaining frosting.

Chocolate Velvet Frosting

Makes enough to fill and frost two 9-inch layers

1½ cups sugar
6 tablespoons cornstarch
¼ teaspoon salt
1½ cups boiling water
3 squares unsweetened chocolate
¼ cup (½ stick) butter or margarine
1 teaspoon vanilla

1 Combine sugar, cornstarch, and salt in a medium-size saucepan; stir in boiling water until well blended.

2 Cook, stirring constantly, until mixture thickens. Add chocolate squares and butter or margarine; continue cooking and stirring until chocolate and butter melt; remove from heat; stir in vanilla.

3 Pour into a medium-size bowl; chill, stirring several times, until thick enough to spread.

Fabulous Fudge Cake

Bake at 375° for 25 to 30 minutes. Makes three 9-inch layers

3 squares unsweetened chocolate
2¼ cups sifted cake flour
2 teaspoons baking soda
½ teaspoon salt
½ cup (1 stick) butter or margarine
2¼ cups (1 pound) firmly packed brown sugar
3 eggs
2 teaspoons vanilla
½ cup buttermilk
1 cup boiling water
CHOCOLATE-CREAM FROSTING (recipe follows)

1 Grease bottoms of three 9x1½-inch layer-cake pans; line pans with wax paper; grease paper.

2 Melt chocolate in small saucepan over *very low* heat; save for Step 5.

3 Sift cake flour, baking soda, and salt onto wax paper.

4 Cream butter or margarine in large bowl with spoon or electric mixer at medium speed; gradually add sugar; beat until mixture is fluffy.

5 Beat in eggs, 1 at a time; beat until thick; stir in vanilla and chocolate with spoon or mixer at low speed.

6 Add sifted dry ingredients, a third at a time, alternately with buttermilk, stirring by hand or with mixer at low speed just until blended; stir in boiling water. Pour into pans.

7 Bake in moderate oven (375°) 25 to 30 minutes, or until centers spring back when lightly pressed with fingertip.

8 Cool in pans on wire racks 5 minutes; loosen around edges with knife; turn out onto racks; remove wax paper; cool completely. Put layers together and frost.

Chocolate-Cream Frosting

Makes enough to fill and frost three 9-inch layers

2 squares unsweetened chocolate
2 tablespoons butter or margarine
1 cup sifted 10X (confectioners' powdered) sugar
¼ teaspoon salt

416

1 egg
1 cup cream for whipping
1 teaspoon vanilla

1 Melt chocolate and butter or margarine in top of large double boiler over hot, *not boiling,* water; beat in sugar, salt, and egg until smooth.
2 Place top of double boiler over ice in large bowl; start beating mixture with electric mixer or rotary beater, gradually adding cream; continue beating 3 to 4 minutes, or until fluffy-thick; stir in vanilla.
3 Keep frosting over ice as you work. Chill cake until serving time.

Burnt Sugar Chocolate Cake
Bake at 350° for 40 minutes. Makes three 8-inch layers

2½ cups sifted cake flour
½ cup dry cocoa (not a mix)

2 teaspoons baking soda
½ teaspoon salt
1 tablespoon vinegar
1 cup milk
1 cup soft vegetable shortening
2 cups sugar
2 eggs
½ cup hot water
1 teaspoon vanilla
   BURNT SUGAR FROSTING (recipe follows)

1 Grease and flour three 8x1½-inch layer-cake pans; tap out excess flour.
2 Sift flour, cocoa, baking soda, and salt onto wax paper; reserve. Stir vinegar into milk to sour in a cup; reserve.
3 Beat shortening, sugar, and eggs in large bowl of mixer at high speed 3 minutes.
4 Stir in dry ingredients alternately with soured milk, beating after each addition until batter is smooth. Stir in hot water and vanilla; pour batter onto prepared cake pans.

Calling all chocolate lovers: (left to right): Burnt Sugar Chocolate Cake, Breton Chocolate Cake and super-luscious Hungarian Chocolate Squares.

5 Bake in moderate oven (350°) 40 minutes, or until centers spring back when lightly pressed with fingertip.
6 Cool layers in pans on wire racks 10 minutes; loosen around edges with a knife; turn out onto wire racks; cool completely.
7 Put layers together with BURNT SUGAR FROSTING; frost sides and top with remaining frosting; drizzle with reserved syrup.

Burnt Sugar Frosting
Makes enough to frost three 8-inch layers

¾ cup granulated sugar
¾ cup boiling water
¾ cup (1½ sticks) butter or margarine
2 egg yolks
6 cups sifted 10X (confectioners' powdered) sugar

1 Spread granulated sugar in a large heavy skillet; heat very slowly until sugar melts and starts to turn deep golden; add water slowly, stirring constantly. Continue heating until melted sugar dissolves completely in water. Boil syrup rapidly two minutes longer; cool completely.
2 Beat butter or margarine until smooth in a medium-size bowl; add yolks; blend well.
3 Reserve 2 tablespoons of the cooled syrup for decorating cake; add remaining syrup alternately with 10X sugar to butter mixture; beat until smooth and spreadable.

Breton Chocolate Pound Cake
Bake at 300° for 1 hour and 45 minutes. Makes one 9-inch tube cake

5 squares unsweetened chocolate
1⅓ cups water
2 cups sifted all-purpose flour
2 cups sugar
1 teaspoon salt
½ cup (1 stick) butter or margarine
3 eggs
1 teaspoon aromatic bitters
1 teaspoon vanilla
2 teaspoons baking powder
CHOCOLATE GLAZE (recipe follows)

1 Combine chocolate and water in a small saucepan. Heat, stirring constantly, until chocolate melts; cool until lukewarm.
2 Sift flour, sugar, and salt into large bowl of

Fabulous Fudge Cake, blanketed with creamy chocolate frosting and wreathed with fresh golden walnut meats.

electric mixer; cut in butter or margarine with a pastry blender to make a crumbly mixture.
3 Add cooled chocolate mixture. Beat at medium speed for 5 minutes. Chill batter in bowl for at least 1 hour.
4 Return bowl to mixer. Beat at medium speed 1 minute. Add eggs, 1 at a time, beating 1 minute after each addition. Add aromatic bitters and vanilla and beat 2 minutes. Add baking powder and beat 2 minutes more.
5 Pour batter into a greased 8-cup fancy tube pan which has been lightly dusted with dry cocoa (or a 9x5x3-inch loaf pan).
6 Bake in slow oven (300°) 1 hour and 45 minutes, or until a toothpick inserted in center comes out clean. Cool cake in pan on wire rack 10 minutes; loosen around edges with a knife. Turn cake out of pan on a wire rack and cool completely.
7 Frost with CHOCOLATE GLAZE and garnish with sliced almonds, if you wish.

CHOCOLATE GLAZE: Break up 1 package (4 oz.) sweet cooking chocolate; heat with 1 tablespoon butter and three tablespoons water over moderate heat, stirring until melted. Off heat, beat in 1 cup 10X (confectioners' powdered) sugar, a dash salt and 1 teaspoon vanilla. Makes ½ cup.

Hungarian Chocolate Squares
(Rigó Jancsi)
Bake at 350° for 15 minutes. Makes 12 servings

Cake
3 squares unsweetened chocolate
4 eggs, separated
½ cup superfine sugar
¾ cup (1½ sticks) butter or margarine
⅔ cup sifted cake flour
¼ teaspoon salt
1 teaspoon vanilla

Filling
10 squares semisweet chocolate (from two 8-ounce packages)
2 cups cream for whipping
2 tablespoons coffee liqueur

Frosting
1 cup superfine sugar
½ cup hot coffee
6 squares semisweet chocolate
2 tablespoons light corn syrup
2 tablespoons butter or margarine
2 tablespoons coffee liqueur

1 To make cake: Melt chocolate in top of a double boiler over hot water; cool to lukewarm.
2 Grease a 15x10x1-inch baking pan; line with wax paper; grease paper.
3 Beat egg whites until foamy-white and double

419

in volume in a medium-size bowl. Beat in ¼ cup of the sugar, 1 tablespoon at a time, until meringue stands in soft peaks.

4 Beat butter or margarine in a large bowl; gradually add remaining ¼ cup sugar and continue beating until mixture is well-blended. Beat in egg yolks until smooth, then cooled chocolate. Sift flour and salt into chocolate mixture; stir to blend; add vanilla.

5 Stir ⅓ of the meringue mixture from Step 3 into chocolate mixture; fold in remaining meringue mixture until well-blended. Spread batter evenly in prepared pan.

6 Bake in moderate oven (350°) 15 minutes, or until top springs back when lightly touched with fingertip.

7 Cool in pan on wire rack for 5 minutes; loosen cake around edges of pan with a sharp knife; invert cake onto a large cooky sheet; peel off wax paper; invert cake onto a large cake rack; cool completely.

8 Make filling: Cut semisweet chocolate into small pieces. Combine with cream in a medium-size saucepan. Heat slowly, stirring constantly, until chocolate melts; remove from heat; stir in coffee liqueur. Pour into a medium-size bowl. Chill 1½ hours, or until mixture is completely cold.

9 Beat chilled chocolate-cream mixture until stiff and thick.

10 Cut cooled cake in half crosswise. Place 1 half on a small cooky sheet. Top with whipped chocolate cream, spreading to make a layer about 1½ inches thick; top with second half of cake. Chill at least 1 hour, or until filling is firm.

11 Make frosting: Heat sugar and coffee in a medium-size saucepan until sugar dissolves. Cut chocolate into small pieces; add to saucepan with corn syrup. Heat to boiling, stirring constantly; cook, at a slow boil, stirring constantly, 5 minutes. Remove from heat; add butter or margarine and coffee liqueur. Beat 5 minutes, or until mixture begins to thicken. Quickly spread over cake layer about ¼-inch thick. Chill at least 1 hour.

12 To serve: Cut cake into 12 squares with a heavy sharp knife; decorate each square, if you wish.

420

Marble Crown Cake
Pamper both white- and chocolate-cake fans with this rich buttery teaser that takes only a shower of sugar for frosting

Bake at 375° for 1 hour. Makes one 9-inch tube cake

    2½ cups sifted all-purpose flour
    2 teaspoons baking powder
    ¼ teaspoon salt
    4 eggs, separated
    1 cup (2 sticks) butter or margarine
    1½ cups sugar
    ⅔ cup milk
    ⅛ teaspoon grated orange rind
    ¼ teaspoon orange extract
    ¼ cup dry cocoa (not a mix)
    ¼ cup water
    2 tablespoons 10X (confectioners' powdered) sugar

1 Grease a 10-cup tube mold or 9-inch angel-cake pan well; dust lightly with flour, then tap out.

2 Sift flour, baking powder, and salt onto wax paper.

3 Beat egg whites until they stand in firm peaks in a large bowl; set aside for Step 5.

4 Cream butter or margarine in a large bowl with spoon or electric mixer at medium speed; add sugar gradually, beating until fluffy. Beat in egg yolks, 1 at a time, until fluffy.

5 Add sifted dry ingredients, a third at a time, alternately with milk, stirring with a spoon or beating with mixer at low speed just until blended. Fold in beaten egg whites until no streaks of white remain.

6 Spoon half of batter into a second bowl; stir in orange rind and orange extract.

7 Blend cocoa and water in a cup; fold into batter in first bowl.

8 Spoon batters, alternating chocolate and white, into bottom of prepared pan to make a layer. Repeat with remaining batters to make 2 more layers, alternating white over chocolate and chocolate over white each time. *Do not stir the batters in pan.*

9 Bake in moderate oven (375°) 1 hour, or until top springs back when lightly pressed with fingertip.

10 Cool in pan on wire rack 5 minutes. Loosen around edge and tube with knife; turn out onto rack; cool completely.

11 When ready to serve, sift 10X sugar over cake; place on serving plate. Cut in thin slices with a sharp knife.

Birthday Year Cake
Bake this fudgy cake in a jelly-roll pan, cut into pieces, and fit together to form the numeral of your birthday child's age.

Bake at 375° for 35 minutes. Makes 20 servings

For Marble Crown Cake, butter-rich chocolate and orange batters are swirled and baked together in a decorative mold.

3 squares unsweetened chocolate
2¼ cups sifted cake flour
2 teaspoons baking soda
½ teaspoon salt
½ cup (1 stick) butter or margarine
2¼ cups (1 pound) firmly packed light brown sugar
3 eggs
2 teaspoons vanilla
½ cup buttermilk
1 cup boiling water
1 jar (12 ounces) jelly
BOILED CHOCOLATE FROSTING (recipe follows)

1 Grease baking pan, 15x10x1; line with wax paper; grease paper.
2 Melt chocolate in small saucepan over *very low* heat; set aside for Step 4.
3 Sift cake flour, baking soda, and salt onto wax paper.
4 Cream butter or margarine with brown sugar until fluffy in large bowl with spoon or electric mixer at medium speed. Beat in eggs, one at a time, beating well after each; stir in vanilla and melted chocolate.
5 Add sifted dry ingredients, a third at a time, alternately with buttermilk, stirring by hand or with mixer at low speed, just until blended; stir in boiling water. Pour into prepared pan.
6 Bake in moderate oven (375°) 35 minutes, or until top springs back when lightly pressed with fingertip.

7 Cool in pan on wire rack 5 minutes; loosen around edges with knife; turn out onto rack; peel off paper; cool completely.
8 To assemble cake: Trim crusts, then cut cake lengthwise into five even-size strips; cut each strip in half. Spread five strips with your birthday child's favorite-flavor jelly, then top each with a plain one. Arrange on serving tray or cooky sheet, following *diagram below,* to form the numeral you wish.

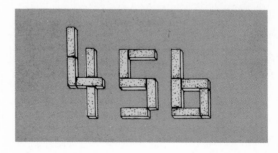

9 Make BOILED CHOCOLATE FROSTING. Spread on top and sides of cake. Decorate with birthday-cake candles.

Boiled Chocolate Frosting
Soft, smooth, and glossy—a bit like pudding
Makes about 3½ cups, or enough for a birthday numeral cake

421

2 cups sugar
½ cup cornstarch
½ teaspoon salt
2 cups boiling water
4 squares unsweetened chocolate
6 tablespoons (¾ stick) butter or margarine
2 teaspoons vanilla

1 Mix sugar, cornstarch, and salt in medium size saucepan; stir in boiling water slowly.
2 Cook slowly, stirring constantly, until mixture thickens and boils 3 minutes. Add chocolate and butter or margarine; continue stirring, keeping over low heat, just until chocolate melts and is well-blended. Remove from heat; stir in vanilla.
3 Pour into medium-size bowl; chill, stirring several times, until creamy-smooth and easy to spread.

Blue-Ribbon Chocolate Cake

A real winner! After baking, layers are split and put back together with fruit filling. Frosting is sweet, dark, and rich
Bake at 350° for 35 minutes. Makes one 9-inch 6-layer cake

2¾ cups sifted cake flour
2½ teaspoons baking powder
½ teaspoon salt
1 cup (2 sticks) butter or margarine
1½ cups sugar
2 teaspoons rum flavoring or extract
½ teaspoon vanilla
4 eggs
2 package (4 ounces each) sweet cooking chocolate, melted
1¼ cups milk
FRUIT-NUT FILLING (recipe follows)
FUDGE FROSTING (recipe follows)
Walnut halves

1 Grease three 9x1½-inch layer-cake pans; line bottoms with wax paper; grease paper.
2 Sift flour, baking powder, and salt onto wax paper or foil.
3 Cream butter or margarine in a large bowl with spoon or electric mixer at medium speed; add sugar gradually, beating until fluffy. Beat in rum flavoring or extract and vanilla.
4 Beat in eggs, one at a time, until fluffy, then slowly beat in melted chocolate.
5 Add sifted flour mixture, a third at a time, alternately with milk, stirring with a spoon or beating with mixer at low speed just until blended. Pour into prepared pans, dividing evenly.

6 Bake in moderate oven (350°) 35 minutes, or until centers spring back when lightly pressed with fingertip.
7 Cool in pans on wire racks 5 minutes; loosen around edges with a knife; turn out onto racks; peel off wax paper; cool layers completely.
8 While layers bake and cool, prepare FRUIT-NUT FILLING and FUDGE FROSTING.
9 Split each cake layer with a long-blade knife. Put back together, alternately with FRUIT-NUT FILLING and FUDGE FROSTING on a serving plate; frost side and top of cake with remaining frosting, making swirls with the tines of a fork. Decorate with walnut halves.

FRUIT-NUT FILLING—Beat 1 egg in the top of a double boiler; blend in 1 cup sugar, 1 tablespoon flour, 1 cup (8-ounce carton) dairy sour cream, and ½ cup chopped seedless raisins. Cook, stirring often, over simmering water 15 minutes, or until thick. Cool about 30 minutes, then stir in ½ cup chopped walnuts, ½ teaspoon vanilla, and ¼ teaspoon grated lemon rind; chill.

FUDGE FROSTING—Melt 4 squares unsweetened chocolate with 4 tablespoons (½ stick) butter or margarine in the top of a small double boiler over simmering water; remove from heat. Sift 1 package (1 pound) 10X (confectioners' powdered) sugar into a medium-size bowl; beat in ½ cup milk, 1 teaspoon rum flavoring or extract, and a dash of salt until smooth, then stir in melted chocolate mixture. Let stand, stirring once or twice, until thick enough to spread.

Brownstone Front Cake

Bake at 325° for 1 hour and 15 minutes. Makes one 9x5x3-inch loaf

2 squares unsweetened chocolate
1 cup boiling water
2¼ cups sifted cake flour
1 teaspoon baking soda
1 teaspoon ground cinnamon
⅛ teaspoon salt
½ cup (1 stick) butter or margarine
1⅔ cups firmly packed brown sugar
2 eggs
1 teaspoon vanilla
½ cup buttermilk

1 Pour boiling water over chocolate in a small bowl; stir until melted; cool. Reserve for step 4.
2 Grease a 9x5x3-inch loaf pan; dust lightly with flour, tapping out any excess flour.

3 Sift flour, baking soda, cinnamon, and salt onto wax paper.

4 Beat butter or margarine, sugar, and eggs in large bowl of mixer at high speed 3 minutes. Beat in vanilla and cooled chocolate mixture. Remove bowl from mixer.

5 Stir in flour mixture alternately with buttermilk, beating after each addition until batter is smooth. Pour into prepared pan.

6 Bake in slow oven (325°) 1 hour and 15 minutes, or until center springs back when lightly pressed with fingertip.

7 Cool cake in pan 10 minutes on wire rack. Loosen around edges with a knife; turn out onto wire rack; cool completely.

QUICK BOWL METHOD CAKES

Busy-Day Cake

This layer cake, made the easy one-bowl way and frosted in the pan, is great for a family dessert . . . or add a few ingredients to change it into a spicy Peach Upside-Down Cake.
Bake at 350° for 30 minutes. Makes one 9x9x2-inch cake

    2 cups sifted cake flour
1¼ cups sugar
2½ teaspoons baking powder
    1 teaspoon salt
½ cup soft vegetable shortening
¾ cup milk
    2 eggs
1½ teaspoons vanilla
    COCOA FROSTING (recipe follows)

1 Grease a 9x9x2-inch baking pan; lightly dust with flour; tap out any excess.

2 Combine flour, sugar, baking powder, salt and shortening in a medium-size bowl; stir in milk until blended; beat at medium speed with electric mixer for 2 minutes; add eggs and vanilla; beat another 2 minutes. Spread batter evenly in prepared pan.

3 Bake in moderate oven (350°) 30 minutes, or until center springs back when lightly pressed with fingertip. Cool cake in pan on wire rack. Spread with COCOA FROSTING.

Cocoa Frosting

Beat 3 tablespoons softened butter or margarine with ⅓ cup dry cocoa until well-blended; stir in 2 cups sifted 10X (confectioners' powdered) sugar alternately with 3 tablespoons milk until smooth and spreadable; stir in ½ teaspoon vanilla and ¼ teaspoon salt.

Peach Upside-Down Cake

Juicy peaches in a butterscotch sauce make this delicious variation of the basic cake.
Bake at 350° for 45 minutes. Makes one 13x9x2-inch cake

    1 recipe Busy-Day Cake
⅓ cup butter or margarine
⅔ cup firmly packed light brown sugar
¼ teaspoon ground cloves
    1 can (about 1 pound) sliced peaches, well drained

Way to dress up a humble loaf cake: top with peaches.

1 Melt butter or margarine in bottom of a 13x9x2-inch baking pan in moderate oven (350°); stir in brown sugar and cloves; spread mixture to coat bottom of pan evenly. Arrange peach slices in a pattern over sugar mixture.

2 Prepare cake batter as directed in BUSY-DAY CAKE; spread evenly over peach slices.

3 Bake in moderate oven (350°) 45 minutes, or until center springs back when lightly pressed with fingertip. Loosen edges of cake with knife; invert immediately onto serving plate; let stand one or two minutes; lift off pan; serve cake warm.

Applesauce Cake

Bake at 350° for 40 minutes. Makes one 13x9x2-inch cake

    1 cup seedless raisins, chopped
½ cup chopped nuts
    3 cups sifted cake flour
1½ cups sugar
1½ teaspoons baking soda
½ teaspoon salt
½ teaspoon ground cinnamon
¼ teaspoon ground allspice
¼ teaspoon ground cloves
¾ cup soft vegetable shortening

423

1 jar (15 ounces) applesauce (1½ cups)
2 eggs
1 teaspoon vanilla

1 Grease a 13x9x2-inch baking pan; dust lightly with flour; tap out any excess.
2 Toss raisins and nuts with 1 tablespoon of the flour in a small bowl; reserve.
3 Sift remaining flour, sugar, baking soda, salt, cinnamon, allspice, and cloves into large bowl of mixer. Add shortening and applesauce. Beat at medium speed for 2 minutes. Add eggs and vanilla. Beat at medium speed for 1 minute.
4 Stir in raisin-nut mixture until well-blended; pour into prepared pan.
5 Bake in moderate oven (350°) 40 minutes, or until center springs back when lightly pressed with fingertip.
6 Cool cake in pan on wire rack 10 minutes; loosen around edges with a knife; turn out onto wire rack; cool completely.
7 Cut into squares and serve with whipped cream, ice cream or lemon sauce, if you wish.

Lady Baltimore Cake
(Silver Cake)
Bake at 350° for 30 minutes. Makes two 9-inch layers

2⅔ cups sifted cake flour
1½ cups sugar
 4 teaspoons baking powder
 1 teaspoon salt
 ⅔ cup soft vegetable shortening
1¼ cups milk
 1 teaspoon vanilla
 4 egg whites
   PINK MOUNTAIN CREAM FROSTING (See Lord Baltimore Cake, White Mountain Cream Frosting)
   LADY BALTIMORE FILLING (recipe follows)

1 Grease bottoms of two 9x1½-inch layer-cake pans; line pans with wax paper; grease and flour paper; tap out any excess.
2 Combine flour, sugar, baking powder, salt, shortening, ¾ cup milk, and vanilla in the large bowl of mixer; (lining pans makes it easier to remove delicate cake). Beat at low speed until blended, then beat at high speed for 2 minutes. Add remaining ½ cup milk and egg whites; continue beating at high speed, scraping down side of bowl often, 2 minutes longer; pour batter into pans.
3 Bake in moderate oven (350°) 30 minutes,

or until centers spring back when lightly pressed with fingertip.
4 Cool layers in pans on wire racks 10 minutes; loosen around edges with a knife; turn out onto wire racks; remove wax paper; cool completely.
5 Put layers together with LADY BALTIMORE FILLING; frost side and top with PINK MOUNTAIN CREAM FROSTING. Decorate with maraschino cherry halves and pecan halves, if you wish.

Lady Baltimore Filling
Makes enough filling for two 9-inch layers

 ½ cup finely chopped pecans
 ⅓ cup cut-up dried figs
 ⅓ cup chopped raisins
 3 tablespoons chopped maraschino cherries
 2 teaspoons grated orange rind
1½ cups PINK MOUNTAIN CREAM FROSTING

1 Combine pecans, figs, raisins, cherries, and orange rind in a medium-size bowl; toss to mix well.
2 Fold in PINK MOUNTAIN CREAM FROSTING until well blended.

Golden Meringue-Topped Cake
Bake at 350° for 35 minutes, then at 400° for 8 minutes. Makes one 13x9x2-inch cake

2¼ cups sifted cake flour
1½ cups granulated sugar (for cake)
 3 teaspoons baking powder
 1 teaspoon salt
 2 eggs
 ½ cup soft vegetable shortening
 1 cup milk
 1 teaspoon vanilla
   BROWN SUGAR MERINGUE (recipe follows)
 ½ cup chopped pecans
 ½ cup flaked coconut

1 Grease a 13x9x2-inch baking pan; dust lightly with flour; tap out any excess.
2 Sift flour, sugar, baking powder, and salt into large bowl of mixer; add eggs, shortening, milk, and vanilla. Blend at low speed ½ minute, then 2 minutes at high speed, scraping bowl frequently with rubber scraper. Pour into prepared pan.
3 Bake in moderate oven (350°) 35 minutes, or until center springs back when lightly touched with fingertip.
4 Prepare BROWN SUGAR MERINGUE while cake is baking. Spread quickly on hot cake; sprinkle with nuts and coconut.
5 Bake in hot oven (400°) 8 minutes or until top is golden brown.

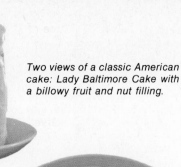

Two views of a classic American cake: Lady Baltimore Cake with a billowy fruit and nut filling.

Brown Sugar Meringue
Makes enough meringue for one 13x9x2-inch cake

2 egg whites
1 tablespoon lemon juice
1 cup firmly packed brown sugar

1 Beat egg whites in a small bowl until foamy-white and double in volume; beat in lemon juice.
2 Beat in sugar, 1 tablespoon at a time, until meringue stands in peaks.

Strawberries And Cream Cake
(Whipped Cream Cake)
Bake at 350° for 30 minutes. Makes two 9-inch layers

2⅔ cups sifted cake flour
1½ cups sugar
  2 teaspoons baking powder
  ¼ teaspoon salt
1⅓ cups cream for whipping
  4 eggs
1½ teaspoons vanilla
    STRAWBERRY BUTTER CREAM FROSTING (recipe follows)

1 Grease two 9x1½-inch layer-cake pans; dust lightly with flour; tap out any excess.
2 Measure flour, sugar, baking powder, and salt into a sifter; reserve.
3 Beat cream in a medium-size bowl until stiff; reserve.
4 Beat eggs in a small bowl until very thick and light; beat in vanilla; fold into reserved whipped cream. Sift dry ingredients over cream mixture; gently fold in until batter is smooth; pour batter into prepared pans.
5 Bake in moderate oven (350°) 30 minutes, or until centers spring back when lightly pressed with fingertip.
6 Cool layers in pans on wire racks 10 minutes; loosen around edges with a knife; turn out onto wire racks; cool completely.
7 Put layers together with STRAWBERRY BUTTER CREAM FROSTING; frost side and top with remaining frosting; garnish with strawberries (from frosting), if you wish.

Strawberry Butter Cream Frosting
Makes enough to fill and frost two 9-inch layers

  1 pint strawberries
½ cup (1 stick) butter or margarine
  1 pound sifted 10X (confectioners' powdered) sugar

1 Mash enough strawberries to measure ⅓ cup.
2 Beat butter or margarine in a medium-size bowl until soft; beat in mashed strawberries. Add 10X sugar slowly; beating until smooth.

425

What the perfect sponge cake should look like: tall and golden with an ever-so-fine-and-feathery texture.

FOAM CAKES

426

The family of *FOAM CAKES* (sponge, angel and chiffon cakes to name three) includes all those whose main leavening is the air which has been beaten into the egg whites. As the cake bakes, the air expands and the batter around it expands, and, presto! the cake rises.

SPECIAL TIPS FOR FOAM CAKES

To keep your foam cakes light and airy, after you have beaten the egg whites to perfection, always *fold* in dry ingredients. Use rubber scraper in a circular motion. Slowly, down through the batter, across the bottom, up the

opposite side, and across the top, to bring some of the batter up and over the egg whites.

When using mixer for folding in flour mixture, use *low* speed once you start adding flour, to keep tender texture.

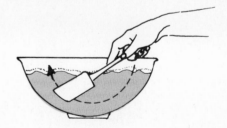

Our Best Sponge Cake
Bake at 325° for 1 hour. Makes one 9-inch tube cake

6 eggs
1 cup sifted cake flour
½ teaspoon salt
1 cup sugar
1 teaspoon vanilla

1 Separate eggs, one at a time, into a custard cup, then place whites in a large bowl and yolks in a medium-size bowl. The tiniest bit of yolk in the whites will keep them from beating up, and that's why it's good practice to use a custard cup first. Eggs separate easiest while cold from the refrigerator, but after separating, let them stand at room temperature to warm so they will beat up to their highest volume.
2 Measure cake flour and salt into a sifter set on wax paper.

3 Beat egg whites until foamy-white and double in volume with an electric mixer at high speed. Beat in ½ cup of the sugar, 1 tablespoon at a time, until meringue forms soft peaks. Your test: Peaks will be just stiff enough to bend slightly as the beater is raised.
4 Beat egg yolks until thick and lemon-colored with mixer at high speed, then beat in the remaining ½ cup sugar, 1 tablespoon at a time, until mixture is very thick and fluffy. Raise the beater again, and the yolk mixture should run off in a very thick stream. Beat in vanilla.
5 Sift flour mixture into egg-yolk mixture all at once, then fold in. Using a rubber scraper or wooden spoon, turn batter over and over gently from bottom of bowl until flour is blended in completely. Work with a light touch to keep the mixture fluffy.
6 Add egg-yolk mixture to meringue, then fold in until no streaks of white or yellow remain. Batter should be airy and fluffy-light.
7 Pour batter into an ungreased 9-inch tube pan. The ungreased side gives the cake a wall to climb on during baking. Run a small spatula or knife through batter to spread it evenly and bring any large air bubbles to the top. (If the air is left in, the baked cake will have tiny holes or tunnels in it.)
8 Bake cake in slow oven (325°) 1 hour, or until top springs back when lightly pressed with fingertip and cake is richly golden.
9 Cake should cool in its pan, so turn it upside down and hang the tube over an unopened quart-size soft drink bottle; let cool completely.
10 To turn out, loosen cake around edge and tube with a knife; invert onto a wire rack, then turn right side up. Leave plain or sprinkle top with 10X (confectioners' powdered) sugar. Cut

cake into wedges, using a sawing motion with a sharp knife, or pull apart into wedges with two forks.

Old-Fashioned Sponge Cake
Bake at 325° for 1 hour. Makes one 9-inch tube cake

1 cup sifted cake flour
1 teaspoon baking powder
½ teaspoon salt
6 eggs, separated
1 cup sugar
1 teaspoon orange extract
½ teaspoon lemon extract

1 Sift flour, baking powder, and salt onto wax paper; reserve.
2 Beat egg whites in large bowl of mixer at high speed until foamy-white and double in volume. Beat in ½ cup of the sugar, 1 tablespoon at a time, until meringue stands in soft peaks.
3 Beat egg yolks in small bowl of mixer at high speed until thick and lemon color. Beat in remaining ½ cup of the sugar, 1 tablespoon at a time, until mixture is very thick and fluffy. Beat in orange and lemon extract.
4 Fold flour, ⅓ at a time, into egg yolk mixture with a wire whip or rubber scraper until completely blended.
5 Fold flour-egg-yolk mixture into meringue until no streaks of white or yellow remain. Pour into an ungreased 9-inch tube pan.
6 Bake in slow oven (325°) 1 hour, or until top springs back when lightly pressed with fingertip.
7 Invert pan, placing tube over a quart-size soft-drink bottle; let cake cool completely. Loosen cake around the edge and the tube and down the sides with a spatula. Cover pan with a serving plate; shake gently; turn upside down; lift off pan. Sift 10X sugar over top, if you wish, and serve with sweetened fruit.

Old-Fashioned Jelly Roll
Bake at 400° for 10 minutes. Makes 8 servings

½ recipe OUR BEST SPONGE CAKE (recipe precedes)
3 tablespoons 10X (confectioners' powdered) sugar
1½ cups any fruit jelly

1 Grease a 15x10x1-inch baking pan; line bottom with wax paper cut ½ inch smaller than pan; grease paper.
2 Prepare batter for OUR BEST SPONGE CAKE; spread evenly in prepared pan.
3 Bake in hot oven (400°) 10 minutes, or until

center springs back when lightly pressed with fingertip.

4 Loosen cake around edges with a knife; invert onto a clean towel sprinkled with 1 tablespoon 10X sugar; peel off wax paper. Starting at a short end, roll up cake, using towel to lift and guide it; wrap in towel; cool completely.

5 Unroll cake carefully. Spoon jelly over cake, spreading to make an even layer. Reroll cake, not in towel, and let stand about ½ hour before cutting. Dust with remaining 10X sugar, slice and serve.

Rosette Ribbon Torte
Makes 12 servings

HOT-MILK SPONGE CAKE (recipe follows)
   WALNUT-MERINGUE ROUNDS AND ROSETTES (recipe follows)
6 squares semisweet chocolate
¾ cup (1½ sticks) butter or margarine
1 tablespoon instant coffee powder
4 egg yolks (from Walnut-Meringue Rounds and Rosettes)
1 package (1 pound) 10X (confectioners' powdered) sugar, sifted
1 cup cream for whipping
½ cup raspberry preserves

1 Make Hot-Milk Sponge Cake and Walnut-Meringue Rounds and Rosettes. Wrap sponge layers tightly in foil or transparent wrap and store in cupboard for one or two days. Place meringue layers in separate containers; cover loosely. Store in a dry place where layers won't be bumped or broken.

2 Melt 4 squares of the chocolate in the top of a small double boiler over hot water. Drop from the tip of a teaspoon onto a wax-paper-lined cooky sheet to form small rounds; chill until firm.

3 At least 6 hours before serving, melt remaining 2 squares chocolate, following directions in Step 2. Combine chocolate with butter or margarine, instant coffee, and egg yolks in a large bowl; beat until fluffy. Slowly beat in 10X sugar until smooth.

4 Beat cream until stiff in a bowl.

5 Layer dessert this way: Place one sponge layer on a large serving plate; spread half of the whipped cream over top; cover with a meringue layer. Carefully spoon raspberry preserves over meringue. Top with second meringue layer; spread with remaining cream;

cover with second sponge layer. Frost sides of dessert with part of the butter-cream mixture.

6 Attach a star tip to a pastry bag; spoon remaining butter cream into bag. Press out in rosettes over top of dessert to cover completely, then around bottom edge.

7 Carefully loosen chocolate rounds from wax paper; press part into frosting on top of dessert and remainder around bottom; tuck meringue rosettes in between. Sprinkle top with more 10X sugar, if you wish. Chill dessert until serving time.

●

Walnut-Meringue Rounds and Rosettes
Bake at 300° for 35 minutes. Makes two 7-inch layers and 12 rosettes

½ cup ground walnuts
½ cup sifted cornstarch
4 eggs
¼ teaspoon cream of tartar
1 cup sugar
1 teaspoon vanilla

1 Grease a large cooky sheet; flour lightly, tapping off any excess. Draw two 7-inch circles on sheet. (A saucer makes a good guide.)

2 Mix walnuts and cornstarch in a small bowl.

3 Separate eggs, placing whites in a large bowl and yolks in a cup to chill for making frosting.

4 Add cream of tartar to egg whites. Beat until foamy-white and double in volume. Beat in sugar, a tablespoon at a time; until sugar dissolves completely and meringue stands in firm peaks; fold in walnut mixture and vanilla.

5 Attach a star tip to a pastry bag; spoon meringue into bag. Press out 12 small rosettes onto cooky sheet. Pipe remaining meringue, dividing evenly, into circles on cooky sheet to form layers. (Layers will spread slightly during baking.)

6 Bake in slow oven (300°) 35 minutes, or until firm and lightly golden. Cool completely on cooky sheets on wire racks. Loosen carefully from cooky sheets with a spatula; slide off onto racks.

●

Hot-Milk Sponge Cake
Bake at 350° for 25 minutes. Makes two 8-inch layers

1 cup sifted cake flour
1 teaspoon baking powder
¼ teaspoon salt
3 eggs
1 cup sugar
¼ cup hot milk
1 teaspoon vanilla

1 Grease two 8x1½-inch round layer-cake pans; flour lightly, tapping out any excess.

2 Sift flour, baking powder, and salt onto wax paper.

3 Beat eggs in large bowl of electric mixer at high speed until fluffy-thick; slowly beat in sugar until mixture almost doubles in volume and is very thick. Turn speed to low; beat in hot milk and vanilla.

4 Fold in flour mixture, a third at a time, just until blended. Pour into prepared pans.

5 Bake in moderate oven (350°) 25 minutes, or until centers spring back when lightly pressed with fingertip. Cool 10 minutes in pans on wire racks; loosen carefully around edges with a knife; turn out onto racks. Cool completely.

●

Choco-Peach Cake

Fluffy fruit filling hides beneath the snowy cream frosting and chocolate topping on this three-layer beauty

Bake at 375° for 15 minutes. Makes 8 servings

1 *recipe* OUR BEST SPONGE CAKE (recipe precedes)
1 *package (10 ounces) frozen sliced peaches, thawed*
2 *tablespoons thawed frozen concentrated orange juice*

An unusual way to trim a cake: with jewels of brittle.

A particularly high and handsome cake: sponge-based Rosette Ribbon Torte.

429

An Americanization of the famous Hungarian Dobos Torta: Chocolate-Brittle Torte with amber candy top.

¼ teaspoon vanilla
⅛ teaspoon almond extract
1 envelope unflavored gelatin
2 eggs separated
3 tablespoons sugar
2 cups cream for whipping
½ cup semisweet-chocolate pieces (from a 6-ounce package)
2 teaspoons vegetable shortening

1 Grease three 8x1½-inch layer-cake pans; line with wax paper; grease paper.
2 Prepare batter for OUR BEST SPONGE CAKE; pour into prepared pans, dividing evenly.
3 Bake in moderate oven (375°) 15 minutes, or until centers spring back when pressed with fingertip.

4 Cool in pans on wire racks 5 minutes; loosen around edges with a knife; turn out onto racks. Peel off paper; cool layers completely.
5 Drain syrup from peaches into a 1-cup measure. Press fruit through a sieve into a small bowl or beat until smooth in an electric blender and place in a bowl; stir in orange juice, vanilla, and almond extract.
6 Soften gelatin in ¼ cup of the peach syrup in the top of a small double boiler. Beat egg yolks slightly in a small bowl; stir into gelatin mixture. Cook, stirring constantly, over simmering water 3 to 5 minutes, or until gelatin dissolves and mixture coats a metal spoon; strain into a large bowl. Stir in peach mixture. Chill 20 minutes, or until as thick as unbeaten egg white.

7 While peach mixture chills, beat egg whites until foamy-white and double in volume in a small bowl; beat in sugar, 1 tablespoon at a time, until sugar dissolves completely and meringue stands in firm peaks. Beat ½ cup of the cream until stiff in a second small bowl. (Set remaining cream aside for frosting in Step 12.)

8 Fold whipped cream, then meringue into thickened gelatin mixture until no streaks of white or yellow remain.

9 Cut a 7-inch round from center of one cooled cake layer and lift out, leaving a ½-inch-wide ring. (Wrap round cutout to use for nibbles or another dessert.)

10 Place ring on a whole layer on a serving plate; spoon peach mixture into ring; top with remaining whole layer. Chill at least 2 hours.

11 Melt semisweet-chocolate pieces with shortening in a cup over simmering water; spread on top of cake. Chill again until chocolate is firm.

12 Just before serving, beat remaining 1½ cups cream until stiff in a medium-size bowl; spread on side of cake. (Or attach a large star tip to a pastry bag; fill bag with whipped cream and press out around cake, using an up-and-down motion, as pictured.) Garnish plate with peach slices, if you wish. Cut into wedges with a sharp knife.

●

Alaska Cream Log
Strawberry and pistachio ice creams fill this feathery-light sponge roll
Bake at 400° for 10 minutes, then at 425° for 5 minutes. Makes 8 servings

½ *recipe* OUR BEST SPONGE CAKE (recipe precedes)
1 *tablespoon 10X (confectioners' powdered) sugar*
1 *pint strawberry ice cream, slightly softened*
1 *pint pistachio ice cream, slightly softened*
4 *egg whites*
¾ *cup granulated sugar*
1 *teaspoon vanilla*

1 Grease a 15x10x1-inch baking pan; line bottom with wax paper cut ½ inch smaller than pan; grease paper.

2 Prepare batter for OUR BEST SPONGE CAKE; spread evenly in prepared pan.

3 Bake in hot oven (400°) 10 minutes, or until center springs back when lightly pressed with fingertip.

4 Loosen cake around edges with a knife; invert onto a clean towel sprinkled with 10X sugar; peel off wax paper. Starting at a short end, roll up cake, using towel to lift and guide it; wrap in towel; cool completely.

5 Unroll cake carefully. Spoon strawberry ice cream lengthwise over one half and pistachio ice cream over the other half, spreading each to make an even layer. Reroll cake; wrap in foil. Freeze several hours, or until very firm.

6 About 20 minutes before serving time, beat egg whites until foamy-white and double in volume in a large bowl; sprinkle in granulated sugar, 1 tablespoon at a time, beating all the time until sugar dissolves completely and meringue forms soft peaks; beat in vanilla.

7 Unwrap cake roll; place on a cooky sheet. Frost with meringue, spreading it to bottom edge and making deep ridges with spatula.

8 Bake in hot oven (425°) 5 minutes, or until meringue is toasty-golden. Lift roll onto a serving plate with two pancake turners; cut crosswise into about-1-inch-thick slices.

Chocolate-Brittle Torte
What a creation! Six thin cake layers are filled with dark chocolate cream, then topped with shattery caramel candy
Bake at 350° for 20 minutes. Makes 12 servings

1½ *cups sifted cake flour*
½ *teaspoon baking powder*
½ *teaspoon salt*
6 *eggs*
1 *teaspoon cream of tartar*
1½ *cups sugar*
¼ *cup water*
1 *teaspoon vanilla*
1 *teaspoon lemon extract*
CHOCOLATE CREAM (recipe follows)
CREAM CARAMEL BRITTLE (recipe follows)
Walnut halves

1 Grease bottoms of three 9x1½-inch layer-cake pans; line with wax paper; grease paper.

2 Measure cake flour, baking powder, and salt into sifter.

3 Separate eggs, placing whites in a large bowl; place 3 yolks in a second large bowl. Save remaining 3 yolks in a cup for CHOCOLATE CREAM.

4 Beat egg whites with cream of tartar until foamy-white and double in volume; sprinkle in 1 cup sugar *very slowly*, 1 tablespoon at a time, beating all the time until meringue forms soft peaks.

5 Stir water into the 3 egg yolks in large bowl; beat until thick. Beat in remaining ½ cup sugar, 1 tablespoon at a time, until fluffy, then beat in vanilla and lemon extract.

431

6 Sift dry ingredients over egg-yolk mixture and fold in, then fold in meringue until no streaks remain.

7 Measure 1⅓ cups of batter into each of the prepared pans; spread to edges to make thin layers. (Cover remaining batter for baking 3 more layers.)

8 Bake layers in moderate oven (350°) 20 minutes, or until golden and centers spring back when lightly pressed with fingertip. Remove from pans; peel off wax paper; cool on racks.

9 Wash pans; grease and line with wax paper. Make 3 more layers from remaining batter, following Steps 7 and 8.

10 Make CHOCOLATE CREAM. Put layers together with ½ cup between each on serving plate; keep remaining filling at room temperature. Chill cake while making candy topping.

11 Make CARAMEL BRITTLE; pour slowly over top of cake, spreading quickly to edge. (It hardens fast, so be speedy.) Frost side of cake with remaining CHOCOLATE CREAM, making deep swirls with knife. Decorate with walnut halves. Chill until serving time. (Torte is best and cuts more neatly if chilled overnight.)

12 When ready to serve, crack candy topping by tapping along cutting lines with a sharp heavy-blade knife, then slice into serving-size wedges.

CARAMEL BRITTLE—Melt ¾ cup granulated sugar over low heat in small heavy saucepan, stirring often with a wooden spoon, *just until golden.* (Watch it, for sugar will turn brown quickly.) Pour over cake at once.

Chocolate Cream
Delectably rich and buttery. Recipe makes both filling and frosting
Makes 3½ cups

    3 egg yolks (from Chocolate-Brittle Torte)
    2 tablespoons water
    ½ cup sugar
    4 squares unsweetened chocolate
    1 tablespoon rum extract or flavoring
    1 teaspoon vanilla
    1 cup (2 sticks) butter or margarine
    1 cup cream for whipping

1 Beat egg yolks with water until thick in medium-size bowl; beat in sugar, 1 tablespoon at a time, until fluffy.

2 Melt chocolate in top of double boiler over simmering water; stir in egg mixture. Cook, stirring constantly, about 1 minute, or until mixture thickens; remove from heat. Beat in rum extract or flavoring and vanilla; cool slightly.

3 Cream butter or margarine in medium-size bowl; beat in chocolate mixture *very slowly.*

(Mixture will be thin, but will thicken as cream is folded in.)

4 Beat cream until stiff in small bowl; fold into chocolate mixture until no streaks of white remain.

Star-Bright Cream Cake
Pumpkin and spice and everything nice go into this delicate chiffonlike cake filled and topped with fluffy cream
Bake at 325° for 1 hour and 15 minutes. Makes one 10-inch tube cake

    2 cups sifted flour
    1½ cups granulated sugar
    3 teaspoons baking powder
    1 teaspoon salt
    1 teaspoon pumpkin-pie spice
    1 cup egg whites (about 7)
    ½ teaspoon cream of tartar
    6 egg yolks
    ½ cup canned pumpkin
    ½ cup vegetable oil
    ½ cup water
    2 cups cream for whipping
    2 tablespoons 10X (confectioners' powdered) sugar
    1 teaspoon vanilla

1 Sift flour, 1 cup of the granulated sugar, baking powder, salt, and pumpkin-pie spice into a large bowl.

2 Beat egg whites with cream of tartar until foamy-white and double in volume in a second large bowl; sprinkle in remaining ½ cup granulated sugar, a tablespoon at a time, beating all the time until meringue stands in firm peaks. Set aside for Step 4.

3 Stir egg yolks, pumpkin, vegetable oil, and water into flour mixture until blended, then beat with mixer at medium speed just until smooth.

4 Fold into meringue until no streaks of white remain. Pour into an ungreased 10 inch tube pan.

5 Bake in slow oven (325°) 1 hour and 15 minutes, or until top springs back when lightly pressed with fingertip.

6 Invert pan, placing tube over a soda-pop bottle and let cake cool completely.

7 Loosen around edge and tube with knife; turn out onto a wire rack.

8 About 2 hours before serving, beat cream with 10X sugar and vanilla until stiff in a medium-size bowl.

Towering a full four layers, Star-Bright Cream Cake is a chiffon-cake type. Its secret ingredients are pumpkin and zippy pumpkin-pie spice.

9 Split cake into four even layers; put back together with about ¼ of the whipped cream; place on a serving plate; spoon remaining cream in puffs on top. Chill. Garnish with tiny ginger "stars," if you wish.

Note: To make ginger "stars," cut tiny shapes from crystallized ginger with a truffle cutter or tiny cookie cutter; stick onto wooden picks.

Buche De Noel
Bake at 375° for 12 to 15 minutes. Makes 12 servings

1 cup sifted cake flour
¼ cup cocoa powder
1 teaspoon baking powder
¼ teaspoon salt
3 eggs
1 cup granulated sugar
⅓ cup water
1 teaspoon vanilla
   10X (confectioners' powdered) sugar
   COFFEE CREAM FILLING (recipe follows)
   CHOCOLATE BUTTER FROSTING (recipe follows)

1 Grease a baking pan, 15x10x1; line with wax paper cut ½ inch smaller than pan; grease paper.
2 Sift flour, cocoa, baking powder, and salt onto wax paper.
3 Beat eggs until thick and creamy in a medium-size bowl; beat in granulated sugar, 1 tablespoon at a time, beating all the time until mixture is very thick. Stir in water and vanilla;

433

fold in flour mixture. Spread batter evenly in prepared pan.

4 Bake in moderate oven (375°) 12 to 15 minutes, or until center springs back when lightly pressed with fingertip.

5 Cut around cake about ¼ inch from edge of pan with a sharp knife; invert pan onto a clean towel dusted with 10X sugar; peel off wax paper. Starting at a long side, roll up cake, jelly-roll fashion; wrap in towel; cool completely on a wire rack.

6 Unroll cake carefully; spread with COFFEE CREAM FILLING; reroll. Place on a serving plate.

7 Cut a ½-inch-thick slice from one end of cake roll; remove inner coil and reshape tightly to form a "knot" on a log; frost with a bit of CHOCOLATE BUTTER FROSTING. Frost cake roll with remaining frosting; draw the tines of a fork lengthwise through frosting to resemble "bark"; press "knot" onto side. Sprinkle ends of roll with chopped pistachio nuts, dust top with 10X sugar, and decorate plate with MINIATURE MERINGUE MUSHROOMS (recipe follows), if you wish.

8 Chill until serving time. Cut crosswise into thick slices.

COFFEE CREAM FILLING—Combine 1 cup cream for whipping, 1 tablespoon instant coffee powder and ½ cup sifted 10X (confectioners' powdered) sugar in a medium-size bowl; beat until stiff.

An old French Christmas classic: Buche de Noel.

CHOCOLATE BUTTER FROSTING—Melt 4 tablespoons (½ stick) butter or margarine and 2 squares unsweetened chocolate in the top of a double boiler over hot, not boiling, water; cool slightly. Combine 2 cups sifted 10X (confectioners' powdered) sugar, ¼ cup milk, and ½ teaspoon vanilla in a medium-size bowl; slowly beat in chocolate mixture until frosting is smooth and easy to spread.

●

Miniature Meringue Mushrooms
Bake at 250° for 30 minutes. Makes 2 dozen

2 egg whites
⅛ teaspoon cream of tartar
½ teaspoon almond extract
⅔ cup sugar
¼ cup semisweet-chocolate pieces

1 Grease two large cookie sheets; flour lightly, tapping off any excess.

2 Beat egg whites, cream of tartar, and almond extract until foamy-white and double in volume in a small bowl.

3 Sprinkle in sugar, 1 tablespoon at a time, beating all the time until sugar dissolves completely and meringue stand in firm peaks.

4 Attach a plain tip to a pastry bag; spoon meringue into bag. To make mushroom caps, press out meringue in 1½-inch rounds; smooth top of each, if needed, with a knife but do not flatten. To make stems, hold pastry bag upright, then press out meringue, pulling straight up on bag for about 1½ inches.

5 Bake in very slow oven (250°) 30 minutes, or until firm but not brown. Let stand several minutes on cookie sheets. Loosen carefully with a small knife; remove to wire racks; cool completely.

6 Melt chocolate in a cup over hot water.

7 Working carefully, make a small hollow in the underside of each cap with the tip of a wooden-spoon handle. Fill hollow with melted chocolate; press stem into hollow. Let stand until chocolate is firm. Sprinkle tops with cocoa, if you wish. Store in a tightly covered container in a dry place.

●

Mocha Log
Perfect choice for February 12. Cake is chocolate; filling, coffee
Bake at 350° for 25 minutes. Makes 8 servings

4 eggs
¾ cup sugar
½ teaspoon vanilla
¼ cup sifted flour
¼ cup dry cocoa (not a mix)

434

Mocha Log, sprinkled with chocolate shavings, is light as a cloud under its slathering of Coffee Cream.

¼ teaspoon baking powder
¼ teaspoon salt
COFFEE CREAM (recipe follows)

1 Beat eggs in a medium-size bowl; beat in sugar gradually until mixture is thick; stir in vanilla. Sift dry ingredients together and fold in. Pour into a greased and wax-paper-lined jelly-roll pan, 15x10x1.
2 Bake in moderate oven (350°) 25 minutes, or until top springs back when lightly pressed. Turn cake out onto a clean towel sprinkled with more sugar; peel off paper. Roll up cake, wrap in towel, cool.

●

When Making Mocha Log:
Work quickly in rolling up the warm cake, lifting towel from the back to make the cake roll and keep it from cracking. Once it's started, you'll be surprised how easily the cake just turns over and over—almost by itself. Wrap the towel tightly around the cake and let it stand to cool completely.

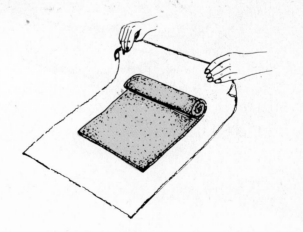

435

Spicy Prune Roll makes a festive showing with a harlequin design of prune filling and whipped cream.

Coffee Cream
Makes 4 cups

2 cups cream for whipping
¼ cup 10X (confectioners' powdered) sugar
4 teaspoons instant coffee powder
1 teaspoon vanilla
    Chocolate curls

1 Beat cream with 10X sugar, instant coffee powder, and vanilla until stiff in a large bowl.
2 Unroll cake carefully; spread evenly with half of the cream mixture; reroll. Frost with remaining cream mixture; sprinkle with chocolate curls. Chill roll 1 hour, or until serving time. Slice crosswise into about-1-inch-thick servings.
Note: To make chocolate curls, shave thin slices from a square of unsweetened chocolate with a vegetable parer.

Spicy Prune Roll
A thick, flavorful prune filling enlivens this inexpensive cake
Bake at 400° for 13 minutes. Makes 10 servings

¾ cup sifted cake flour
1 teaspoon baking powder
½ teaspoon ground cinnamon
¼ teaspoon salt
4 eggs
¾ cup granulated sugar
1 teaspoon vanilla
    10X (confectioners' powdered) sugar
    Prune Filling (recipe follows)
    Whipped cream (optional)

1 Grease a 15x10x1-inch baking pan; line with wax paper cut to fit; grease paper.

2 Measure flour, baking powder, cinnamon and salt into a sifter.

3 Beat eggs until foamy in a medium-size bowl; gradually beat in granulated sugar until mixture is very thick and light (this step is very important). Stir in vanilla.

4 Sift dry ingredients over egg mixture; gently fold in until no streaks of flour remain. Spread batter evenly in prepared pan.

5 Bake in hot oven (400°) 13 minutes, or until center springs back when lightly pressed with fingertip.

Rio Roll is a double chocolate, double threat to dieters. Cake part is sponge-light, filling velvety smooth.

6 Loosen cake around sides of pan; turn upside down onto clean towel dusted with 10X sugar; cut off crisp cake edges with a sharp knife. Starting at short end, gently roll up cake with towel; cool, seam side down.

7 To serve, unroll carefully; remove towel; spread cake with PRUNE FILLING, reserving 3 tablespoons for top decoration, if you wish; reroll. Decorate cake roll with whipped cream rosettes and reserved filling, if you wish. To serve: Cut crosswise into 10 slices.

PRUNE FILLING—Combine 2 cups pitted prunes with 1 cup water in a small saucepan; simmer, covered, 25 minutes; purée prunes with remaining cooking liquid, part at a time, in blender (or press through a sieve). Stir in 2 tablespoons sugar, 1 tablespoon lemon juice, and ½ teaspoon ground cinnamon. Chill. Makes about 1⅔ cups.

●

Rio Roll
Sponge-light cake is filled and frosted with the smoothest chocolate cream imaginable
Bake at 350° for 25 minutes. Makes 8 servings

⅓ cup sifted all-purpose flour
⅓ cup dry cocoa powder (not a mix)
½ teaspoon baking powder
¼ teaspoon salt
4 eggs
¾ cup sugar
1 teaspoon vanilla
1 package (4½ -ounces) chocolate-flavor whipped-dessert mix
½ cup milk
½ cup water
½ cup cream for whipping
Chocolate curls

437

1 Grease a 15x10x1-inch baking pan; line with wax paper; grease paper.

2 Measure flour, cocoa, baking powder, and salt into sifter.

3 Beat eggs until fluffy-thick and lemon-colored in a large bowl; sprinkle in sugar, 1 tablespoon at a time, beating all the time until mixture is very thick. (Beating will take about 10 minutes in all with an electric beater.)

4 Stir in vanilla; sift flour mixture over top, then fold in. Spread batter evenly in prepared pan.

5 Bake in moderate oven (350°) 25 minutes,

or until top springs back when lightly pressed with fingertip.

6 Cut around cake about ¼ inch from edge of pan with a sharp knife; invert pan onto a clean towel dusted with dry cocoa; peel off wax paper. Starting at one end, roll up cake, jelly-roll fashion; wrap in towel. Cool cake completely on a wire rack.

7 While roll cools, prepare whipped-dessert mix with milk and water, following label directions; chill.

8 One hour before serving, beat cream until stiff in a small bowl. Spoon half of the chilled chocolate mixture into a small bowl; beat until smooth; fold in cream.

9 Unroll cake carefully; spread evenly with chocolate-cream mixture; reroll. Place on a serving plate.

10 Beat remaining chocolate mixture until smooth; spread over side and top of roll; sprinkle with chocolate curls. Chill until serving time. Cut crosswise into 8 thick slices. (To make chocolate curls, shave thin strips from a square of unsweetened chocolate with a vegetable parer or a sharp thin-blade knife.)

Angel Food Cake
Bake at 350° for 50 to 60 minutes. Makes one 10-inch tube cake

    1 cup sifted cake flour
1¾ cups sifted sugar
    11 egg whites (1½ cups) at room temperature
1¼ teaspoons cream of tartar
    ¼ teaspoon salt
    1 teaspoon vanilla
    ¼ teaspoon almond extract

1 Sift the flour with half of the sugar (¾ cup plus 2 tablespoons) onto wax paper; reserve.

2 Beat egg whites with cream of tartar and salt in large bowl of mixer at high speed until foamy-white and double in volume. Beat in remaining ⅞ cup sugar, 1 tablespoon at a time, until meringue stands in soft peaks.

3 Fold flour mixture, ¼ at a time, into egg white mixture with a wire whip or rubber scraper until no streaks of dry ingredients remain. Fold in vanilla and almond extract. Pour into an ungreased 10-inch tube pan.

4 Bake in a moderate oven (350°) for 50 to 60 minutes or until tops spring back when lightly pressed with fingertip.

5 Invert pan, placing tube over a quart-size soft drink bottle; let cake cool completely. Loosen cake around the edge and the tube and down

the sides with a spatula. Cover pan with a serving plate; shake gently; turn upside down; lift off pan. Serve as is or, if you wish, with sweetened fruit.

Coffee Chiffon Cake
Bake at 325° for 1 hour and 10 minutes. Makes one 10-inch tube cake

2⅓ cups sifted cake flour
1⅓ cups sugar
    3 teaspoons baking powder
    ½ teaspoon salt
    ½ cup vegetable oil
    5 egg yolks
    ¾ cup cold water
    1 tablespoon instant coffee powder
    1 cup (7 to 8) egg whites
    ½ teaspoon cream of tartar
    MOCHA GLAZE (recipe follows)

1 Sift flour, 1 cup of the sugar, baking powder, and salt into a medium-size bowl. Make a well and add in order: Oil, egg yolks, water, and coffee; beat with a spoon until smooth.

2 Beat egg whites and cream of tartar in large bowl of mixer until foamy-white and double in volume. Beat in remaining ⅓ cup sugar, 1 tablespoon at a time, until meringue stands in firm peaks.

3 Gradually pour egg yolk mixture over beaten whites, gently folding in until no streaks of white remain. Spoon into ungreased 10-inch tube pan.

4 Bake in slow oven (325°) 1 hour and 10 minutes, or until top springs back when lightly pressed in center with fingertip.

5 Invert pan, placing tube over a quart-size soft-drink bottle; let cake cool completely. When cool, loosen cake around outside edge and tube and down sides with a spatula. Cover pan with serving plate; turn upside down; shake gently; lift off pan. Drizzle MOCHA GLAZE over top of cake, letting it run down the side.

Mocha Glaze
Makes enough glaze for top of one 10-inch tube cake

2 tablespoons butter or margarine
2 squares unsweetened chocolate
1 teaspoon instant coffee powder
⅛ teaspoon ground cinnamon
1 cup sifted 10X (confectioners' powdered)
  sugar
2 tablespoons hot water

1 Melt butter with chocolate in a small heavy saucepan over very low heat; stir until blended.
2 Remove from heat; stir in coffee and cinnamon.
3 Add sugar alternately with hot water, beating until smooth.

Marigold Cake
Bake at 375° for 35 minutes. Makes one 10-inch tube cake

1¼ cups sifted cake flour
1½ cups sugar
 10 egg whites (1¼ cups)
1½ teaspoons cream of tartar
 ¼ teaspoon salt
  4 egg yolks

1 teaspoon grated lemon rind
1 teaspoon vanilla

1 Sift flour and ½ cup of the sugar onto wax paper; reserve.
2 Beat egg whites, cream of tartar, and salt in large bowl of mixer at high speed until foamy-white and double in volume. Beat in the remaining 1 cup of sugar, 1 tablespoon at a time, until meringue stands in soft peaks.
3 Fold in flour mixture, ⅓ at a time, with a wire whip or rubber scraper until completely blended.
4 Beat egg yolks in small bowl of mixer at high speed until thick and lemon-color. Beat in lemon rind and vanilla.
5 Fold ½ of the meringue batter into egg yolks until no streaks of white or yellow remain.
6 Spoon batters by tablespoonfuls, alternating colors, into an ungreased 10-inch tube pan. (Do not stir batters in pan.)
7 Bake in moderate oven (375°) 35 minutes, or until top springs back when lightly pressed with fingertip.
8 Invert pan, placing tube over a quart-size soft-drink bottle; let cake cool completely. Loosen cake around the edge and the tube and down the sides with a spatula. Cover pan with a serving plate; turn upside down; shake gently; lift off pan. Cut into wedges and serve with lemon sherbet, if you wish.

439

Angel Food Cake is the daintiest and most delicate of all cakes. Dieter's note: it's also low in calories.

FRUIT CAKES

Q and A on Fruit cakes

Q. I plan to bake fruit cake for gifts. How much can I make at one time with my standard electric mixer?

A. It is best to work with no more than double a recipe and to use your mixer only for creaming the butter or margarine with the sugar and beating in the eggs. For final blending of batter with fruits and nuts, use a preserving kettle or a dishpan as a mixing bowl.

Q. My supermarket sells mixed candied fruits already chopped and ready to mix. May these be substituted for the long list of candied fruits and peels found in so many recipes?

A. Yes. Just use approximately the same cup or weight measure, and, if making a light fruit cake, watch that the mix is made up of all light-color fruits.

Q. Chopping or slicing nuts is such a tedious job. May I put them through the food chopper or twirl them in my electric blender?

A. Both these short cuts will grind the nuts too fine, even to releasing some of their natural oils. So be patient: Chop or slice for best results.

Q. I work at an outside job, so my baking time is limited. Can I start the mixing one evening and finish it the next?

A. Cutting, measuring, and mixing fruits and nuts, plus measuring dry ingredients and even mixing them with the fruits and nuts, can be done ahead, if you wish. And you can grease and line pans beforehand. Then, just before baking, mix batter, combine with fruit mixture, and pour into pans.

Q. I have difficulty baking fruit cake. Sometimes it gets too brown; other times it is not baked so well as I like it. How can I solve these problems?

A. Fruit cakes need a very low temperature—usually 250° to 275°—and the size, shape, and type of pan also dictate baking time. In general, a one-pound loaf will take from two to three hours; an unusually large or deep cake will take a longer baking time. When using a thin-metal pan, line it with a double thickness of wax paper or brown

Who wouldn't welcome receiving one of these fancily decorated, home-baked fruit cakes for Christmas?

paper for extra protection. Some cooks also like to set a pan of water on the bottom of the oven to keep the top of the cake moist and give it a shiny look. Another trick: Lay a sheet of foil or brown paper over cake during the last part of baking to prevent overbrowning.

Q. My recipe calls for wine. What can I substitute for it?

A. Grape juice, sweet cider, or apple or orange juice may be used instead of wine. Grape juice is probably the best substitute in dark fruit cake, although some cooks use coffee for part of the liquid or all of it. In light fruit cakes, cider or fruit juice is a better choice.

Q. What is the best way to store fruit cake?

A. Place the cake in a plastic bag, or wrap in foil or transparent wrap and keep it in the refrigerator no longer than six to eight weeks. For longer storage, wrap as above and freeze.

White Christmas Fruit Cake
Tender white cake fairly glitters with rainbow fruits. Add its fruit topping on serving day
Bake at 275° for 3 hours. Makes one 8-inch tube cake

    3 cups (3 eight-ounce jars) chopped mixed
      candied fruits
    2 cans (3½ ounces each) flaked coconut (2⅔
      cups)
 1½ cups golden raisins
 1½ cups coarsely chopped blanched almonds
 1½ teaspoons grated orange rind
 3¾ cups sifted cake flour
 1½ teaspoons baking powder
  ¾ teaspoon salt
  ¾ cup (1½ sticks) butter or margarine
 1½ cups sugar
    6 eggs
  ½ cup apple juice
  ⅓ cup orange juice
    FRUIT TOPPING (recipe follows)

441

1 Grease bottom and side of an 8-inch tube pan; line bottom with wax paper; grease paper.
2 Combine candied fruits, coconut, raisins, almonds, and orange rind in a large bowl.
3 Sift cake flour, baking powder, and salt over fruit mixture; mix well to coat fruits and almonds evenly.
4 Cream butter or margarine with sugar until fluffy in a medium-size bowl; beat in eggs, one at a time, until creamy-thick; stir in apple and orange juices.

5 Pour over fruit mixture; fold in thoroughly. Spoon batter into prepared pan, pressing down firmly with a spoon to make top even.

6 Bake in very slow oven (275°) 3 hours, or until a long thin skewer inserted near center comes out clean.

7 Cool cake completely in pan on a wire rack. Loosen around edge with a knife; turn out onto rack; peel off paper.

8 To store, slide cake into a plastic bag and seal. It will stay fresh and moist in the refrigerator for about eight weeks, or in freezer for three months. When ready to serve, decorate with FRUIT TOPPING.

FRUIT TOPPING—Mix ¼ cup light corn syrup and ¼ teaspoon grated lemon rind in a 1-cup measure. Cut 1 slice candied pineapple into thin wedges. (You'll need 25 wedges.) Arrange each five around a halved candied red cherry, petal fashion, on cake; carefully spoon syrup over.

Noel Bell Fruit Cake
Bake at 300° for 2 hours. Makes 1 loaf, 9x5x3

    2 cups sifted all-purpose flour
    1 teaspoon baking powder
    1 teaspoon ground cinnamon
    1 teaspoon ground mace
    ½ teaspoon ground cloves
    ¾ cup (1½ sticks) butter or margarine
    ¾ cup firmly packed light brown sugar
    2 eggs
    1 can (1 pound) apricot halves, drained and
       chopped
    ¼ cup Irish whiskey
    2 cups seedless raisins
    1 container (8 ounces) mixed chopped candied fruits
 1½ cups chopped pecans
    1 container (8 ounces) red candied cherries,
       halved
    1 container (4 ounces) green candied cherries, halved
       MARZIPAN (recipe follows)

1 Grease a loaf pan, 9x5x3.

2 Sift flour, baking powder, cinnamon, mace, and cloves onto wax paper.

3 Cream butter or margarine with brown sugar until fluffy-light in a large bowl; beat in eggs, one at a time; stir in apricots and whiskey. Stir in flour mixture until blended, then raisins, mixed fruits, pecans, and cherries. Spoon into prepared pan; spread top even.

4 Bake in slow oven (300°) 2 hours, or until a wooden pick inserted in center comes out clean. Cool completely in pan on a wire rack. Loosen cooled cake around the edges with a knife; turn out onto rack.

5 Wrap cake in wax paper, foil, or transparent wrap; store several days to mellow flavors.

6 Make MARZIPAN. Roll out to a rectangle, ¼ inch thick, on wax paper. Cut out 6 small bell shapes with a 1½-inch cooky cutter; arrange on cake. Pinch off small bits of marzipan trimmings and roll into tiny balls; press onto cake to form clappers for bells. Roll part of remaining trimmings into 6 thin strands; twist each 2 together to form a rope; place on cake at top of bells. (Use any leftover marzipan to stuff into dates or prunes for simple confections.) When ready to serve, cut cake in thin slices.

MARZIPAN—Empty 1 can (8 ounces) almond paste into a medium-size bowl; break up with a fork. Beat 1 egg white slightly in a cup; mix 1 tablespoonful into almond paste, then blend in 1 cup 10X (confectioners' powdered) sugar. Knead mixture in bowl until smooth and stiff enough to handle; knead in a few drops green food coloring to tint lightly.

Marble Fruit Cake
Bake at 300° for 1¾ hours. Makes one 9-inch tube cake

    3 cups sifted all-purpose flour
    2 teaspoons baking powder
    1 teaspoon salt
    ½ teaspoon baking soda
    ½ teaspoon ground cinnamon
    ¼ teaspoon ground ginger
    ¼ teaspoon ground nutmeg
    ⅛ teaspoon ground cloves
    ½ cup chopped dates
    ½ cup chopped walnuts
    ½ cup currants
    1 cup (2 sticks) butter or margarine
    ½ cup firmly packed dark brown sugar
    4 eggs
    ¼ cup currant jelly
    ¼ cup apple juice
    1 container (4 ounces) candied citron,
       chopped
    1 container (4 ounces) candied pineapple,
       chopped
    ¾ cup granulated sugar
    2 teaspoons grated lemon rind
    ¼ cup diced pared fresh lemon sections
       LEMON GLAZE (recipe follows)

1 Generously grease a 9-inch round (12-cup) tube mold; flour lightly, tapping out any excess.

2 Sift 1½ cups of the flour, 1 teaspoon of the baking powder, ½ teaspoon of the salt, ¼ teaspoon of the soda, cinnamon, ginger, nutmeg, and cloves into a medium-size bowl; stir in dates, walnuts, and currants.

3 Cream 1 stick of the butter or margarine with brown sugar until fluffy-light in a large bowl; beat in 2 of the eggs, one at a time, until well-blended; beat in currant jelly.

4 Stir in flour mixture, half at a time, alternately with apple juice, just until blended. Set aside while preparing second batter.

5 Stir remaining 1½ cups flour, 1 teaspoon baking powder, ½ teaspoon salt, and ¼ teaspoon soda into a medium-size bowl; stir in citron and pineapple.

6 Cream remaining 1 stick butter or margarine with granulated sugar until fluffy-light in a large bowl; beat in remaining 2 eggs, one at a time, until well-blended; stir in lemon rind and diced lemon.

7 Stir in flour mixture, half at a time, just until blended. Spoon dark and light batters, alternately, into prepared pan; draw a spatula through the batters to marble.

8 Bake in slow oven (300°) 1¾ hours, or until top springs back when lightly pressed with fingertip. Cool in pan on a wire rack 10 minutes. Loosen around edge and center with a knife; turn out onto rack; cool completely.

9 Wrap cake in wax paper, foil, or transparent wrap; store several days to mellow flavors. Several hours before serving, drizzle LEMON GLAZE over top. Garnish with candied lemon slices and halved candied red cherries, if you wish. Cut into thin wedges.

LEMON GLAZE—Blend 1 cup 10X (confectioners' powdered) sugar with 4 teaspoons lemon juice until smooth in a small bowl. Makes about ⅓ cup.

●

NOTE TO FRUIT CAKE BAKERS

Cakes that are heavy with fruit will keep well in the refrigerator for 8 weeks and in the freezer for at least 3 months. For refrigerator storage, wrap undecorated cake tightly in heavy foil. For freezer storage, wrap cake tightly, then seal in a transparent bag. Label, date, and freeze. Remove from freezer the day before serving or giving and let stand, still wrapped, at room temperature to thaw. Then frost and decorate.

●

Plantation Prune Cake
Bake at 350° for 1 hour and 5 minutes. Makes one 10-inch tube cake

1 jar (1 pound) cooked prunes
2½ cups sifted all-purpose flour

1 teaspoon baking soda
1 teaspoon salt
1 teaspoon ground allspice
1 teaspoon ground cinnamon
1 teaspoon ground nutmeg
1 cup finely chopped pecans
3 eggs
1½ cups sugar
1 cup vegetable oil
½ cup buttermilk
VANILLA GLAZE (recipe follows)

1 Grease a 12-cup tube pan or 10-inch tube pan; flour lightly, tapping out any excess.
2 Drain liquid from prunes into a cup. Pit prunes, then cut each into 3 or 4 pieces; place in a 1-cup measure. Add enough prune liquid to make 1 cup.
3 Sift flour, soda, salt, allspice, cinnamon, and nutmeg into a medium-size bowl; stir in pecans.
4 Beat eggs well in a large bowl; slowly beat in sugar until mixture is fluffy-light. Beat in vegetable oil, then buttermilk; stir in prunes. Beat in flour mixture, a third at a time, until well-blended. Pour into prepared pan, spreading evenly.
5 Bake in moderate oven (350°) 1 hour and 5 minutes, or until top springs back when lightly pressed with fingertip. Cool 10 minutes in pan on a wire rack. Loosen cake around edge and tube with a knife; turn out onto rack; cool completely.

More fruit cakes, dark and light, plain and fancy.

6 Wrap cake in wax paper or transparent wrap, then in heavy foil; freeze up to 8 weeks.

7 The day before serving, remove cake from freezer; let stand, still wrapped, at room temperature to thaw. An hour before serving, unwrap cake; place on a deep plate.

8 Make VANILLA GLAZE; while hot, drizzle slowly over cake, spooning any that drips onto plate back over cake. (Glaze will soak in.) Cut cake into wedges.

VANILLA GLAZE—Combine 1 cup sugar, ½ teaspoon baking soda, ½ cup buttermilk, 1 tablespoon light corn syrup, and ½ cup (1 stick) butter or margarine in a medium-size saucepan. Heat slowly, stirring constantly, to boiling, then cook, stirring constantly, 2 minutes. Remove from heat; stir in 1 teaspoon vanilla.

NOTE: If serving cake without freezing, cover with glaze as soon as cake is removed from pan.

Holiday Dark Fruit Cake
Bake at 275° for 4 hours. Makes one 10-inch tube cake

> 4 cups (2 one-pound jars) chopped mixed candied fruits
> 1 package (15 ounces) seedless raisins
> 1 package (15 ounces) golden raisins
> 1 can (6 ounces) pecans, chopped
> 2½ cups sifted all-purpose flour
> 1 teaspoon baking powder
> 2 teaspoons ground cinnamon
> 1 teaspoon ground mace
> ½ teaspoon salt
> 1 cup (2 sticks) butter or margarine
> 1 cup sugar
> 6 eggs
> ⅓ cup grape jelly
> ½ cup grape juice
> CREAMY FROSTING (recipe follows)

1 Grease bottom and side of a 10-inch tube pan; line bottom with brown paper; grease paper.

2 Combine candied fruits, raisins, and pecans in a very large bowl or kettle. Sift in 1 cup of the flour; stir to coat fruits and nuts well. Save for Step 5.

3 Measure remaining 1½ cups flour, baking powder, cinnamon, mace, and salt into sifter.

4 Cream butter or margarine and sugar until fluffy in large bowl with spoon or electric mixer. Beat in eggs, 1 at a time; blend in grape jelly. Sift in dry ingredients, a third at a time, adding alternately with grape juice. Stir with a spoon or beat with mixer at low speed just until well-blended.

5 Pour batter over fruit-nut mixture; fold and blend until mixed thoroughly. Spoon into prepared pan, pressing down firmly with a spoon to make top even.

6 Bake in very slow oven (275°) 4 hours, or until a long thin metal skewer inserted near center comes out clean. Cool cake completely in pan.

7 Loosen around edge with knife; turn out on wire rack; remove paper. Wrap in wax paper, foil, or transparent wrap, and store in a tightly covered metal container. Cake will keep fresh, moist, and mellow-flavored for several weeks. (Or, if you wish, slide wrapped cake into a plastic bag, seal, then store in your freezer.)

8 Before serving, spread CREAMY FROSTING on top of cake, letting it drip down over side and center hole. Decorate with marzipan fruits, if you wish.

CREAMY FROSTING—Combine 1½ cups sifted 10X (confectioners' powdered) sugar, 2 tablespoons cream, and 1 teaspoon vanilla in 2-cup measure; beat until creamy-smooth. Makes about ¾ cup.

Holly Fruit Loaves
Midget version of the dark classic. Leave plain or frost with 10X sugar icing
Bake at 275° for 1 hour. Makes eight 7-ounce cakes

> 1 jar (1 pound) mixed chopped candied fruits (2 cups)
> 1 package (15 ounces) seedless raisins
> ¾ cup chopped pecans
> 1½ cups sifted all-purpose flour
> 1 teaspoon ground cinnamon
> ½ teaspoon baking powder
> ½ teaspoon ground cloves
> ½ teaspoon salt
> ½ cup (1 stick) butter or margarine
> ½ cup firmly packed dark brown sugar
> 3 eggs
> ¼ cup molasses
> ¼ cup grape juice
> ICICLE GLAZE (recipe follows)

1 Grease eight small loaf pans, 4½x2½x1½; dust lightly with flour.

2 Combine candied fruits, raisins, and pecans in a large bowl. Sift 1 cup of the flour over top; stir lightly to coat fruits and pecans.

3 Sift remaining ½ cup flour, cinnamon, baking powder, cloves, and salt onto wax paper.

4 Cream butter or margarine with brown sugar until fluffy in a medium-size bowl; beat in eggs, one at a time, until fluffy again; stir in molasses. Stir in flour mixture, a third at a time, alternately with grape juice, stirring just until well-blended.

Baked with love, presented with love, this treasury of holiday fruit cakes dressed in Christmas finery.

5 Pour over floured fruit mixture; fold in completely. Spoon into prepared pans, using about ¾ cupful for each and pressing down firmly with spoon to make top even. Place pans, not touching, in a large shallow pan for easy handling. Place a pan of hot water on lower shelf in oven to help keep cakes moist during baking; set cakes on shelf above.

6 Bake in very slow oven (275°) 1 hour, or until a wooden pick inserted in center comes out clean. Cool cakes completely in pans on wire racks. Loosen around edges with a knife; turn out onto racks. Just before serving or giving, drizzle ICICLE GLAZE over each; decorate with red and green candied cherries and angelica, if you wish.

ICICLE GLAZE—Blend 1½ cups sifted 10X (confectioners' powdered) sugar, ¼ cup cream, and 1 teaspoon vanilla in a small bowl; beat until creamy-smooth. Makes about ¾ cup.

Fruit Cake-Ettes

Canned fruit cocktail and a syrup glaze help keep these little cakes moist
Bake at 300° for 55 minutes. Makes eight 6-ounce cakes

½ cup (1 stick) butter or margarine
½ cup firmly packed brown sugar
1 can (8 ounces) fruit cocktail, drained
1 cup golden raisins
½ cup light rum
  OR: ¼ cup orange juice and 1 teaspoon rum flavoring or extract
2 jars (4 ounces each) chopped candied orange peel
2 jars (4 ounces each) chopped candied citron
1 can (5 ounces) toasted slivered almonds
2 eggs, beaten
1¼ cups sifted all-purpose flour
1 teaspoon pumpkin-pie spice
¾ teaspoon salt
½ teaspoon baking powder
¼ cup light corn syrup
  Red and green gumdrops

1 Grease eight tiny angel-cake pans or eight 5-ounce custard cups.
2 Combine butter or margarine, brown sugar, fruit cocktail, raisins, and ¼ cup of the rum (or all of the orange juice and rum extract) in a large saucepan. Heat, stirring constantly, to boiling; pour into a large bowl; cool to lukewarm. Stir in orange peel, citron, almonds, and beaten eggs.
3 Sift flour, pumpkin-pie spice, salt, and baking powder over fruit mixture; fold in just until blended. Spoon into prepared pans, dividing evenly. Place pans, not touching, in a large shallow pan for easy handling. Place a pan of hot water on lower shelf in oven to help keep cakes moist during baking; set cakes on shelf above.
4 Bake in slow oven (300°) 55 minutes, or until

cakes are golden and a wooden pick inserted near center comes out clean. Cool completely in pans on wire racks. Loosen around edges and tubes with a knife; invert onto racks.
5 Combine remaining ¼ cup rum and corn syrup in a small saucepan; heat to boiling; brush over cakes to coat completely. Decorate with flowers of red and green gumdrops.

Miniature Yule Logs

For those who prefer light fruit cake. Juice cans are the handy bakers
Bake at 275° for 1 hour. Makes one dozen 6-ounce cakes

3 jars (4 ounces each) chopped candied pineapple
3 jars (4 ounces each) chopped candied orange peel
1 can (3½ ounces) flaked coconut
1½ cups golden raisins
1 cup coarsely chopped Macadamia nuts
  OR: 1 cup coarsely chopped pecans
2½ cups sifted cake flour
1 teaspoon baking powder
½ teaspoon salt
½ cup (1 stick) butter or margarine
1 cup sugar
4 eggs
½ cup pineapple juice
  PINEAPPLE GLAZE (recipe follows)

1 Grease twelve 6-ounce aluminum fruit-juice cans; dust lightly with flour, tapping out any excess.
2 Combine pineapple, orange peel, coconut, raisins, and nuts in a large bowl.
3 Sift flour, baking powder, and salt over fruit mixture; stir lightly.
4 Cream butter or margarine with sugar until fluffy in a medium-size bowl; beat in eggs, one at a time, until fluffy; stir in pineapple juice. Pour over fruit mixture; fold in completely. Spoon into prepared juice cans, filling each ¾ full and pressing down firmly with spoon to make top even. Stand cans, not touching, in a large shallow pan for easy handling.
5 Bake in very slow oven (275°) 1 hour, or until firm on top and a long metal skewer inserted in center comes out clean.
6 Cool cakes completely in cans on wire racks. Loosen around edges with a knife; turn out onto racks. Just before serving or giving, frost with PINEAPPLE GLAZE. Decorate with colored candied pineapple in designs of your choice.

PINEAPPLE GLAZE—Blend 1½ cups sifted 10X (confectioners' powdered) sugar and ¼ cup pineapple juice in a small bowl; beat until smooth. Makes about ¾ cup.

A sensational way to decorate a cake—with home-baked or store-bought jelly roll slices spiraling round it.

DECORATIVE SPECIAL-OCCASION CAKES

June Rose Wedding Cake
Makes 100 servings
This beauty can be yours with just a little time and some practice. The results are well worth the effort.

Special Items You Will Need
1 three-tier cake pan set
    (7x2¼; 10x2¾; 13x2½ inches)*

2 loaf pans, 9x5x3 inches each
1 five-cup mold
    (6 inches wide, 3 inches deep)
1 cake-decorating set, with:
    Pastry bag; coupling; 6 tubes*
1 plastic turntable, about 15 inches*
3 rounds of heavy cardboard: 14, 10, 7 inches
* *These items available in most large department and hardware stores.*

Preparation Plan
Your cake may be made in three days, following our easy-does-it plan, leaving plenty of time for you for other wedding activities. If you wish to

(continued on page 450)

448

1. For Rosebuds: *For each rose, use a small amount of frosting to secure a two-inch square of wax paper to the top of a small jar. Fill pastry bag with pink frosting. Fit #61 tube into pastry bag. Hold tube so larger end touches center of paper. Gently press frosting out of tube while turning the jar to form the tight center of the bud.*

2. Press out 3 small petals, overlapping around center. Continue to shape 3 to 6 more petals to form a tight, unopened bud.

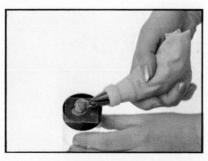

3. For Full-blown Rose: *Fit the #124 tube onto pastry bag. Hold the tube with the wider end touching the center of the paper. Gently press frosting out of the tube, as in Step 1. Center formed with this tube will be slightly open.*

4. Press out 3 petals around the slightly open center. They should partially overlap one another around the center. Then tilt top of tube (the narrow end) outward as you continue to work.

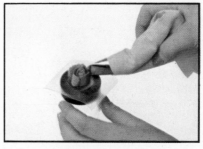

5. Following the same procedure used for the first 3 petals, continue pressing out petals. Shape each additional petal slightly larger than the last. As you continue, you will create the effect of a rose as it would naturally unfold.

6. To finish the full-blown rose, press several more petals around those already formed. Tilt the pastry tube so that these petals slant in a more outward position than any of the others.

449

June Rose Wedding Cake: you can make it.

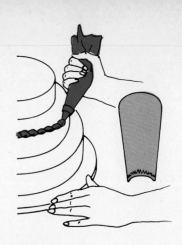

bake, decorate, and freeze the cake two or three weeks before the wedding, be sure to measure your freezer space first. The cake is 14 inches wide and 15 inches tall.

1st day—Bake GROOM'S CAKE; cool; wrap.
2nd day—Bake POUND-CAKE LAYERS
    —Brush all cakes with APRICOT GLAZE
    —Cut and wrap take-home pieces of GROOM'S CAKE
    —Make BRIDAL ROSES
3rd day—Assemble cake

Handy Notes for Baking Cakes

Different sets of cake pans will vary in volume. In the set we used, measuring to the brim, the 13-inch pan holds 24 cups, the 10-inch holds 14 cups, and the 7-inch holds 7 cups. Measure your pans with water to determine the volume of each. Each package of pound-cake mix makes about 3½ cups of batter.

Each pan should be filled half full with batter.

Making the Decorations for the Cake

If this is to be your first experience with a cake decorating set, it would be wise to prepare half the recipe for DECORATOR'S FROSTING and practice the various designs before you start your cake. A little practice and you suddenly become a pro and save that sunny disposition.

Bridal Roses

Prepare DECORATOR'S FROSTING *(recipe follows).* Using half the amount, divide frosting between 2 small bowls. With a few drops of red food coloring, tint one bowl a pale pink and the second bowl a deeper pink. Following the directions that follow, make 36 ROSEBUDS and 30 FULL-BLOWN ROSES.

Allow roses to dry on paper squares on cooky sheet for 2 hours, or until they are firm enough to peel off paper and place on cake.

450

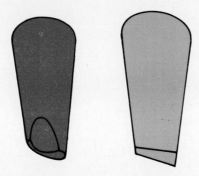

How to Make the Decorative Edgings

You will find your decorating will be more professional if you work out the designs on the frosting with a wooden pick. Then it is simple to follow the design with the pastry bag.

Shell Border—Fit the #98 shell tube onto pastry bag. Press out frosting in overlapping shell design around entire top edge of tier (*see* FIG. 1).

String Scallops—Fit the #2 writing tube onto pastry bag. Mark out scallop pattern in a double scallop. Press out frosting, following design, making single scallop all the way around. Follow with second scallop row to make double scalloping (*see* FIG. 2).

Diamond Pattern—Using same #2 writing tube, follow marked-out pattern, pressing all lines in one direction first, then following with crisscross lines to complete pattern.

Drop Flowers—Fit the #96 drop flower tube or #27 star tube onto pastry bag. Holding the tube about 1/16 inch away from cake, squeeze, relax pressure, pull tube away. Continue all around tier (*see* FIG. 3).

Fluted Scallops—Fit the #27 star tube onto pastry bag. Following marked-out pattern, press out frosting all around tier.

Leaves—Fit the #67 leaf tube onto pastry bag. Press out frosting with a backward and forward motion, then break off pressure with a quick motion to make pointed tip of leaf (*see* FIG. 4).

●

Groom's Cake

The top tier of our wedding cake is made of fruit cake batter. This is the cake that traditionally is saved for the first anniversary. Our recipe makes this cake and two loaf cakes. The loaves are each cut into 25 thin slices and each slice cut in half. These pieces may be packed in wedding cake boxes or wrapped in transparent wrap, then silver paper and tied with silver cord as mementos for the guests.

Bake at 275° from 2 hours, 15 minutes to 2 hours, 45 minutes. Makes one 6x3-inch cake and two 9x5x3-inch loaves

2 jars (1 pound each) mixed candied fruits
1 package (15 ounces) golden raisins
2 cans (3½ ounces each) flaked coconut
2 cups chopped walnuts
2 packages pound cake mix
4 eggs
1 cup liquid
2 tablespoons apricot brandy
    BRANDY-APRICOT GLAZE (recipe follows)

1 Grease generously and flour a round 5-cup mold, 6x3 inches. Grease and line 2 loaf pans, 9x5x3 inches, with wax paper; grease paper.
2 Combine mixed fruits, raisins, coconut, and chopped nuts in a very large bowl or kettle. Add 1½ cups dry pound cake mix and toss to coat fruits and nuts evenly with mix.
3 Prepare pound cake mix with eggs, liquid called for on label, and apricot brandy, following label directions.
4 Pour batter over prepared fruits and nuts and stir gently until evenly mixed.
5 Divide batter among prepared mold and loaf pans. Place one oven rack in center of oven and arrange all three pans on same rack of oven.
6 Bake in very slow oven (275°) for 2 hours, then begin to test cakes. The cakes are done when a cake tester or long wooden skewer is inserted into center of cake and comes out clean. (The cake may be done in another 15 minutes or may take up to 45 minutes longer. The time varies with the brand of cake mix you use and the size and shape of your oven.)
7 Remove layers from oven and cool on wire racks for 30 minutes. Loosen cakes around edges with a thin-blade sharp knife and turn out onto racks; remove wax paper; cool cakes completely. Brush with BRANDY APRICOT GLAZE. *Note:* If not assembling cake at once, you may wrap cooled cakes in foil or transparent wrap; refrigerate or freeze. The cake will stay fresh and moist for one month in the refrigerator and up to three months in the freezer.

●

Pound-Cake Layers

Bake at 325° from 1 hour to 1 hour and 30 minutes. Makes 3 tiers—7-, 10-, and 13-inches each

6 packages pound-cake mix
12 eggs
    Liquid as label directs
3 tablespoons apricot brandy
    BRANDY APRICOT GLAZE (recipe follows)

1 Grease and line tiered cake pans with wax paper; grease paper and then dust with flour, tapping out excess. (An extra step, but very helpful to ensure smooth sides on larger cake layers.)
2 Prepare 2 packages pound cake mix with 4 eggs, liquid called for on label, and 1 tablespoon apricot brandy, following label directions.
3 Pour batter into middle tier pan to half fill the pan. If there is additional batter, pour into largest pan.
4 Repeat Step 2 twice. Pour batter into largest pan to half fill the pan, then half fill the smallest pan. (Any extra batter may be baked as cupcakes for a family treat.)
5 Arrange one oven rack in top third of oven and the second rack in the bottom third of the

451

oven. Place largest cake pan on bottom rack in center of oven. Place middle-size pan at back left of top rack and smallest pan at front right of top rack. (Be sure pans do not touch each other, door, sides, or back of oven.)

6 Bake in slow oven (325°) for 1 hour. Then begin to test layers. The cakes are done when a cake tester or long wooden skewer inserted into the center of each cake layer comes out clean. (Baking times will vary with the width and depth of individual cake pans and also the size and shape of your oven.) All layers should be baked by 1 hour and 30 minutes. If the layers on the top rack are getting too brown but do not test done, cover layers lightly with a piece of foil for the last part of baking.

7 Remove layers from oven and cool on wire racks for 20 minutes. Then line wire racks with towels. Loosen each cake around edge with a thin-blade, sharp knife. Turn cake pan on side and shake layer gently to be sure cake has loosened from pan. Turn out layer onto towel-lined wire rack and peel off wax paper. Cool cake completely. (Towel-lined wire racks make it much easier to handle the larger cakes.)

8 Brush tops and sides of layers with BRANDY-APRICOT GLAZE.

Note: If not assembling cake at once, you may wrap cooled layers in foil or transparent wrap and freeze. Unfrosted cake layers may be frozen for up to three months.

Brandy-Apricot Glaze
Makes about 1¼ cups

1 jar (12 ounces) apricot preserves
¼ cup apricot brandy

Heat apricot preserves until very warm in a small saucepan. Stir in apricot brandy. Strain. The glaze adds flavor to cakes, and helps retain moisture.

Wedding Cake Frosting
Makes enough to frost June Rose Wedding Cake

1 cup (2 sticks) butter or margarine
¾ cup vegetable shortening
3 packages (1 pound each) 10X (confectioners' powdered) sugar
½ teaspoon salt
¼ cup milk
3 tablespoons apricot brandy
3 tablespoons light corn syrup
1 tablespoon vanilla

1 Beat butter or margarine and shortening until soft in a large bowl. Beat in 10X sugar and salt

until mixture is crumbly and all of the sugar has been added.

2 Add milk, brandy, corn syrup, and vanilla. Beat until mixture is smooth and spreadable. *Note:* Keep every bowl of frosting *covered* with a dampened paper towel.

Decorator's Frosting
Makes enough to decorate June Rose Wedding Cake

½ cup (1 stick) butter or margarine
½ cup vegetable shortening
2 packages (1 pound each) 10X (confectioners' powdered) sugar
¼ teaspoon salt
3 tablespoons milk
2 tablespoons apricot brandy
2 tablespoons light corn syrup
1 teaspoon vanilla

1 Beat butter or margarine and shortening until soft in a large bowl. Beat in 10X sugar and salt until mixture is crumbly and all sugar has been added.

2 Add milk, brandy, corn syrup, and vanilla to bowl. Beat until mixture is very thick and smooth.

To Assemble Wedding Cake

1 Place 14-inch cardboard round on turntable. (Cardboard between each layer makes cutting easier.) Center largest POUND-CAKE LAYER on cardboard. Frost top and side thinly with WEDDING CAKE FROSTING.

2 Center 10-inch cardboard round on cake layer and top with middle cake layer; frost. Center 7-inch cardboard round on cake and top with smallest cake layer; frost. Center 6-inch GROOM'S CAKE on top; frost. This thin basic coat of frosting keeps any stray crumbs in place, and provides a smooth base for final frosting. Allow frosting to dry at least one hour.

3 Frost cake all over with a smooth; thick layer of the WEDDING CAKE FROSTING.

4 Follow designs for cake as we decorated it, or work out your own pattern.

5 Put a small amount of DECORATOR'S FROSTING in each of two small bowls; then tint one a pale pink and the other a pale green with red and green food colorings. Reserve.

6 Fit the #98 shell tube on pastry bag; fill bag with part of remaining frosting (either WEDDING or DECORATOR'S). Pipe a large mound of frosting onto the center of top tier of cake. Peel FULL-BLOWN ROSES off wax paper and arrange, alternating shades of pink, onto frosting mound.

7 Press several small mounds of frosting onto middle cake tier; arrange more roses; Building up from these roses, press out mounds of frosting and place roses on cake side going up from this tier level to meet roses on top. (Should roses start to slide, press a new mound of frosting, arrange roses into frosting and hold in place several minutes until frosting begins to set.)

8 Then arrange roses on bottom tier and build up to meet middle tier of roses. Peel ROSEBUDS off wax paper. Pipe a dot of frosting at intervals, following cake design, on bottom and middle tiers, and press in ROSEBUDS.

9 Fit the #27 star tube onto your pastry bag; fill bag with pink frosting. Press out tiny flowers at intervals, following design.

10 Fit the #67 leaf tube onto pastry bag; fill bag with green frosting. Pipe leaves onto cake, following our picture.

Now your cake is ready to serve. If cake is to be served in a day or two, cover loosely with transparent wrap and keep in as cool a place as possible.

If cake is to be frozen, place in freezer just as it is, and allow to freeze until frosting is very firm, then cover cake completely with foil, or transparent wrap. Remove cake from freezer the day before the wedding and remove wrappings. When cake has thawed, it can be lightly covered with transparent wrap.

To Cut Your Wedding Cake

1 Start at bottom tier and remove roses. Cut a 3-inch-wide strip all the way around cake. (Bottom and second tier will now be even.)

2 Slice strip into 1-inch-wide pieces; place on serving plate. Cut roses into pieces and add part to each cake slice.

3 Next cut strip from second tier in the same way and slice.

4 Remove the fruit cake tier and save for the first anniversary. Cut pound cake under fruit cake tier into small wedges, then remove cardboard and slice second pound-cake tier into small wedges. Remove cardboard and cut last layer into small pieces.

To Decorate Ceremonial Cake Cutter

Choose a silver or silver-plated cake or pie server or carving knife. Decorate the handle by winding narrow satin ribbon around and round the handle. Insert tiny lilies of the valley and end with bows and a few strands of ribbon.

Flower Bouquet Cake

Bake at 350° for 25 minutes. Makes two heart-shape layers or two 9-inch layers

  1 *package white cake mix*
   Egg whites
   Water

  ½ *teaspoon almond extract*
  ½ *cup strawberry jam*
  2 *cans (about 1 pound each) ready-to-spread creamy vanilla frosting*
 1¼ *cups sifted 10X (confectioners' powdered) sugar*
   Green, yellow, red, and blue food colorings

1 Grease and line two heart-shape layer-cake pans or two 9x1½-inch layer-cake pans with wax paper. Grease paper.

2 Prepare cake mix with egg whites and water; add almond extract, as directed on label. Pour into prepared pans.

3 Bake in moderate oven (350°) 25 minutes, or until centers spring back when lightly pressed with fingertip.

4 Cool layers in pans on wire racks 10 minutes; loosen around edges with a knife; turn out onto wire racks; peel off wax paper; cool completely.

5 Cut a piece of cardboard the size and shape of cake layers. Place one layer on cardboard; spread strawberry jam evenly over. Top with remaining layer.

6 Tint 1½ cans of the frosting a pale green with food coloring in a medium-size bowl. Frost top and side of cake, reserving some for decoration.

7 Decorating the cake: Make a wax-paper pastry bag: Tear off a 12-inch square of wax paper. Fold it into a double-thick triangle (*see* FIG. 1). Holding each end of long side, curl both towards the third end, pulling tightly until all three corners meet; point at bottom should be closed (*see* FIG. 2). Tape back seam. Fill cone with reserved green frosting. Cut off the tip of cone with scissors to make a ⅛-inch opening (*see* FIG. 3). Continued on page 456

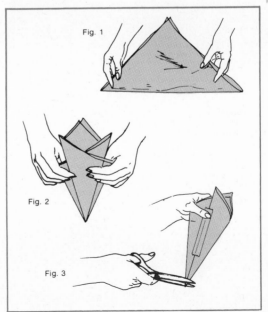

Fig. 1

Fig. 2

Fig. 3

453

454

1. For Lilies of the Valley: *To form stems, press curves of green frosting onto frosted cake with cone.*

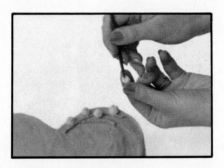

2. Shape tiny bits of white frosting into balls. Using tip of the handle end of a small artist's brush, press a hollow into center of each. Arrange the flowers along stems. Shape tiny centers from yellow frosting; press into hollow of each little flower.

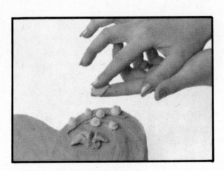

3. For Wild Roses: *For petals of rose, flatten small, equal-size balls of pink frosting with your fingers.*

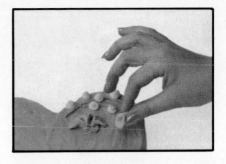

4. Shape by pinching one end of petal with fingers. Arrange 5 petals with pinched ends toward center, on small dot of green frosting to form rose, as shown.

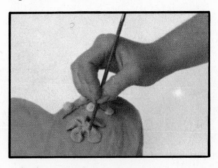

5. To make tiny pockets to hold flower centers, press down centers of roses with tip of brush handle. Shape bits of yellow frosting and arrange in pockets formed in centers of rose.

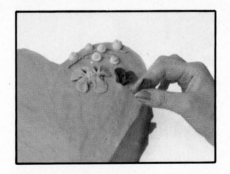

6. For Violets: *Flatten small ball of violet frosting with fingers. Pinch one end as with rose petals. Press 3 petals into a small dot of green frosting on cake, as shown. Add a yellow center. Then pipe green stems on violets.*

455

◀ *Pastel-pretty floral Bouquet Cake.*

8 Make "flower clay" frosting: Work enough 10X sugar into remaining frosting in a bowl until mixture can be shaped with your hands and leaves side of bowl clean. Divide frosting into 4 parts. Tint 1 yellow, 1 pink, and 1 violet, using food colorings. Keep the fourth part white. Wrap each part in transparent wrap to keep frosting from drying. For flowers, follow step-by-step pictures and arrangement (*see pictures that follow*).

9 To complete cake: Press green frosting through wax-paper cone in a zigzag pattern around bottom edge of cake. Dissolve a few drops of green food coloring in a few drops of water in a small bowl. Dip small artist's brush into mixture and brush over flower stems to heighten color.

Party Petits Fours

These dainties start with a rich chiffon cake. Make it a day or two ahead of glazing, frosting, and decorating

Bake at 350° for 30 minutes. Makes 6½ dozen tiny cakes

2¼ cups sifted cake flour
1¼ cups sugar
  3 teaspoons baking powder
  1 teaspoon salt
  2 eggs, separated
⅓ cup vegetable oil
  1 cup milk
  1 teaspoon vanilla

APRICOT GLAZE (recipe follows)
FONDANT FROSTING (recipe follows)
BUTTER CREAM DECORATING FROSTING (recipe follows)

1 Grease a 15x10x1-inch baking pan; line bottom with wax paper; grease paper.
2 Sift cake flour, 1 cup of the sugar, baking powder, and salt into a large bowl.
3 Beat egg whites until foamy-white and double in volume in a medium-size bowl; sprinkle in remaining ¼ cup sugar, 1 tablespoon at a time, beating all the time until meringue forms soft peaks.
4 Blend vegetable oil and ½ cup of the milk into flour mixture, then beat 2 minutes with mixer at medium speed, or 150 strokes by hand. Stir in egg yolks, remaining ½ cup milk, and vanilla; beat 1 minute at medium speed, or 100 strokes by hand. Fold in meringue until no streaks of white remain. Pour into prepared pan.
5 Bake in moderate oven (350°) 30 minutes, or until top of cake springs back when lightly pressed with fingertip.
6 Cool in pan on a wire rack 5 minutes; loosen around edges with a knife; invert onto a large rack or clean towel; peel off wax paper; cool cake completely. Wrap tightly in foil or transparent wrap and store.
7 When ready to frost and decorate, unwrap cake and place on a cutting board; trim crusts. Cut cake into 36 diamonds, 10 squares, 20 rectangles, and 12 one-and-a-half-inch rounds, following diagram below.

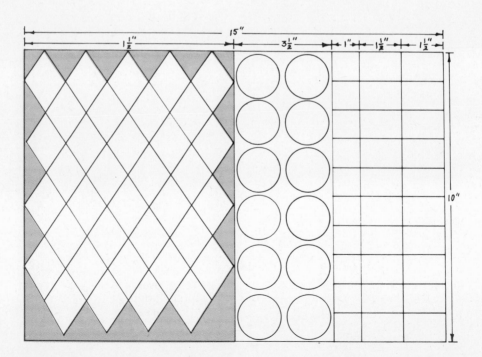

456

Make these designs with flower and leaf tips

Make these designs with a star tip

Make these designs with a plain tip

Make these designs with leaf and rosette tips

Apricot Glaze

This fruity glaze coats the cakes first and sets any loose crumbs
Makes enough to glaze 6½ dozen tiny cakes

1 jar (12 ounces) apricot preserves
1 cup sugar
1 cup water

1 Heat apricot preserves, stirring constantly, until melted in a small saucepan; remove from heat. Press through a sieve into a small bowl, or twirl until smooth in blender.
2 Combine sugar and water in same saucepan; heat, stirring several times, to boiling, then cook, without stirring, to 230° on a candy thermometer. (A small amount of syrup will spin a 2-inch thread when dropped from a spoon.) Stir syrup into sieved preserves.
3 Holding cakes, one at a time, on a fork over bowl, spoon on glaze to cover completely.
4 Place cakes on wire racks set over wax paper or foil; let stand 3 hours, or until sticky-firm.

Fondant Frosting

Use a candy thermometer—don't guess—and frosting will be perfect. Each cake is double-frosted—first with vanilla, then with a second flavor
Makes enough to frost 6½ dozen tiny cakes

3 cups granulated sugar
¼ teaspoon cream of tartar
1½ cups water
1 package (1 pound) sifted 10X (confectioners' powdered) sugar (about 4½ cups)
¼ teaspoon salt
1 teaspoon vanilla
½ teaspoon almond extract
¼ teaspoon lemon extract
  Yellow food coloring
  Few drops peppermint extract
  Red food coloring

1 Combine granulated sugar, cream of tartar, and water in a large saucepan; heat slowly, stirring constantly, until sugar dissolves, then cook, without stirring, to 226° on a candy thermometer; remove from heat.
2 Cool to 125°, then gradually beat in 10X sugar, salt, and vanilla until smooth and syrupy-thick. (It will take from 4 to 4½ cups of sugar.) Measure 1½ cups into a second bowl; set remaining aside for Step 5.
3 Again holding glazed cakes, one at a time on a fork over bowl, spoon on the first layer of frosting to cover completely.
4 Use a wooden pick to slide each cake onto a rack set over wax paper or foil; scrape any frosting that drips onto paper or foil back into bowl. Let cakes stand 2 hours, or until frosting is firm.

457

5 When ready to add final coat of frosting, divide remaining frosting into three custard cups; stir almond extract into one cup; stir lemon extract and a few drops of food coloring to tint frosting pale yellow into the second cup; stir a few drops peppermint extract and red food coloring to tint frosting pale pink into the third cup.

6 Working with a third of the frosted cakes, hold, one at a time, on a fork over almond-frosting cup; spoon frosting, the same as for vanilla coating, over cakes to cover tops and sides completely. (If frosting gets too thick to spoon, stir in a drop or two of hot water.)

7 Repeat Step 6 with remaining plain frosted cakes, covering half of them with lemon frosting and the remaining half with peppermint frosting. Let stand 4 hours, or until frosting is completely dry.

Now prepare decorating frosting and go as simple or as artistic as you wish in decorating these dainty confections.

Butter Cream Decorating Frosting
After mixing frosting, divide into quarters and tint each a different color
Makes enough to decorate 6½ dozen tiny cakes

  ½ cup (1 stick) butter or margarine
3½ cups sifted 10X (confectioners' powdered)
      sugar
  1 egg white
      Red, yellow, and green food colorings

1 Cream butter or margarine in a medium-size bowl; beat in 10X sugar gradually and egg white until frosting is creamy-smooth. Divide into 4 small bowls.
2 Leave one white, and tint each of the others with a drop or two of food colorings to make pink, yellow, and green.
3 Fill a cake-decorating set with frosting, one color at a time; fit with star, leaf, flower, rosette, or plain tip, following manufacturer's directions, and decorate cakes with the designs of your choice.

459

For a dainty ladies' tea, a silver tray full of Petits Fours you can make and decorate yourself.

Cake mix magic—three beauties that begin in boxes: Daffodil Torte (left), Orange Sunburst (center), Almond Fruit Basket (right).

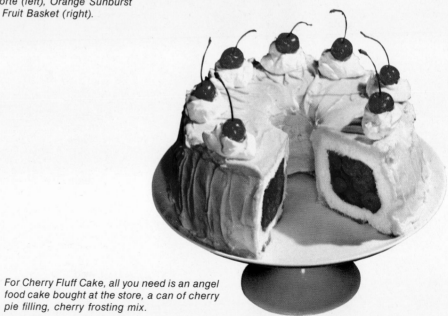

For Cherry Fluff Cake, all you need is an angel food cake bought at the store, a can of cherry pie filling, cherry frosting mix.

CAKES TO BUY AND

BUILD UPON

CAKES TO BUY AND BUILD UPON: YOUR OWN CREATIONS FROM PACKAGE CAKES AND CAKE MIXES

The beauty of packaged cakes, of cake and frosting mixes is that they need not begin and end with the package. They are enormously versatile, can be transformed, with a few added ingredients plus an ounce or two of ingenuity, into lavish cakes with a deceptive "from-scratch" look and flavor. Some cake mixes, given special treatment, emerge not as cakes but as puddings and puffs.

The secret of mixes is simply to use them not as ends in themselves but as ingredients, as short-cuts to recipe classics. It's easily done— the following recipe collection shows just *how* easily.

● ● ●

Cherry Fluff Cake
Makes 6 to 8 servings

1 packaged 8-inch round angel cake
1 can (1 pound, 5 ounces) cherry pie filling
1 package creamy cherry frosting mix

1 Trim a 1-inch-thick slice from top of cake; set aside. Hollow out cake this way: cut a deep circle around top about ¾ inch in from outer edge, then cut a second circle about ¾ inch from center hole. Loosen piece at bottom with a fork and lift out leaving a shell; place shell on a serving plate.
2 Spoon cherry pie filling into shell; replace top slice.

3 Prepare creamy cherry frosting mix with butter or margarine and water, following label directions; frost cake; chill. Cut into wedges; serve plain or with whipped cream.

●

Savannah Cream Ring
Flavored-by-you whipped topping gives purchased cake a homemade touch
Makes 12 servings

1 packaged angel food cake (17 to 22 ounces)
1 container (9 ounces) frozen whipped topping, thawed
½ cup finely chopped pecans
1 teaspoon instant coffee

1 Place cake, smooth side up, on a board. Using a sawing motion with a sharp knife, cut a ½-inch layer from the top; reserve.

2 To hollow cake, cut a deep circle ½ inch from outer edge and a second circle ½ inch from inner edge; remove cake ring in large pieces, loosening at bottom with a fork. (There should be about 2 cups; reserve for nibblers.) Place hollowed cake on serving plate.

3 Mix 2 cups of the whipped topping, ⅓ cup of the pecans, and instant coffee until well-blended in a small bowl; spoon into hollow in cake, packing firmly. Replace top of cake.

4 Frost cake with remaining whipped topping; sprinkle with remaining pecans. Chill at least 4 hours.

Italian Angel Cake
A surprise blending of ricotta cheese and grated chocolate fills angel food layers
Makes 12 servings

1 packaged angel food cake (17 to 22 ounces)
1 pound ricotta cheese
½ cup 10X (confectioners' powdered) sugar, sifted
1 square semisweet chocolate, grated
2 tablespoons Curacao
1 teaspoon vanilla
½ cup candied red cherries, quartered
2 tablespoons chopped toasted almonds

1 Place cake, smooth side up, on a board. Using a sawing motion with a sharp knife, cut cake into 3 even layers.

2 In large bowl of electric mixer, beat cheese on medium speed about 3 minutes, or until smooth; add sugar, chocolate, Curaçao, and vanilla; beat 2 minutes longer. Stir in cherries and almonds.

3 Place bottom layer on serving plate; spread with half the filling; add middle layer; spread with remaining filling; set top layer in place. Chill about 2 hours, or until filling is firm.

Butterscotch Icebox Squares
Whether you call these rich dessert squares pudding or cake—they're great
Makes 12 servings

1 packaged angel food cake (17 to 22 ounces)
2 packages (about 4 ounces each) butterscotch pudding
2⅓ cups milk

1 tall can (14½ ounces) evaporated milk
2 bananas, sliced

1 Cut cake into 1-inch cubes; place in a large bowl.

2 Combine butterscotch pudding, milk, and evaporated milk in a large saucepan; cook, following label directions for pudding. Fold hot pudding into cake until all pieces are evenly coated.

3 Spoon half the pudding mixture into a pan, 13x9x2; add sliced bananas in a single layer; top with remaining pudding mixture, spreading evenly. Place a layer of wax paper directly on pudding. Chill at least 3 hours.

4 To serve, peel off wax paper; cut dessert into squares. Garnish with whipped cream, if you wish.

Rocky Road Rollup
With a little sleight of hand, packaged jelly roll goes homemade fancy in mere minutes
Bake at 400° for 10 minutes. Makes 6 servings

1 can (about 1 pound, 6 ounces) pineapple pie filling
1 packaged jelly roll
¼ cup semisweet chocolate pieces

1 Place pineapple pie filling in a sieve set in a bowl; lift and turn filling over and over with a rubber spatula until most of the thick juice has drained off.

2 Unroll jelly roll; spread evenly with the drained fruit to within ½ inch of edges. Reroll carefully; place, seam side down, on a greased cooky sheet. Brush all over with the thickened juice from pie filling.

3 Bake in hot oven (400°) 10 minutes, or until glaze bubbles; remove roll from oven. Dot top at once with semisweet-chocolate pieces.

4 Lift roll onto a serving plate. Slice and serve warm with vanilla ice cream, if you wish.

Whirligig Pear Cake
Plan to serve this dessert at the table so everyone can see how pretty it is
Makes 4 servings

1 can (about 1 pound) pear halves
¾ cup pear syrup from can
2 tablespoons lemon juice
2 tablespoons brown sugar
1 tablespoon cornstarch
1 sponge layer (2 to a package)

1 Drain and measure syrup from pears; add water, if needed, to make ¾ cup. Add lemon juice.

2 Mix brown sugar and cornstarch in small saucepan; stir in syrup mixture. Cook, stirring constantly, until sauce thickens and boils 3 minutes.

3 Place a sponge layer on deep serving plate (use second layer for lunchbox dessert); arrange drained pears, cut side down, in wheel design on top. Spoon hot sauce over and let soak into cake. Serve warm, cut in wedges.

Double-Berry Cream Cake
Makes 6 servings

2 cups (1 pint) raspberries
2 cups (1 pint) blueberries
¼ cup sugar
1 package sponge layers (2 to a package)
1 pint vanilla ice cream

1 Wash raspberries and blueberries; stem; drain well. Mash ½ cup of the raspberries in a medium-size bowl; stir in sugar. Let stand 15 minutes; stir in remaining berries.

2 Place 1 sponge layer on a serving plate; cover with about ⅓ of the ice cream and half of the berry mixture. Top with remaining cake layer, ice cream, and berries. Cut into wedges.

Viennese Snacks
Rich morsels of pound cake with apricot glaze and luscious frosting
Makes 27 little cakes

½ cup apricot preserves
¼ cup granulated sugar
7 tablespoons water
1 packaged frozen pound cake (12 ounces), thawed
¼ cup dry cocoa (not a mix)
2 tablespoons dark corn syrup
2 tablespoons butter or margarine
2 cups 10X (confectioners' powdered) sugar

1 Combine apricot preserves, granulated sugar, and 4 tablespoons water in a small saucepan; heat to bubbling; cook 2 minutes; press through a sieve.

2 Cut cake in thirds both crosswise and lengthwise to make nine pieces, then cut each piece into thirds to make 27 little bar-shaped cakes. Place on racks over wax paper. Spoon apricot glaze over tops.

3 Combine cocoa, remaining 3 tablespoons water, corn syrup, and butter or margarine in a small saucepan; heat slowly, stirring constantly, until butter is melted. Remove from heat; beat in 10X sugar. Spoon over cakes several times. Sprinkle tops with sliced almonds, if you wish.

CAKE MIX MAGIC

Almond Fruit Basket
Almond-studded angel cake with a center of unusual interest: Peaches, bananas, and pineapple laced with kirschwasser
Bake at 350° for 45 minutes. Makes one 10-inch tube cake

1 package angel-cake mix
  Water
1 can (about 14 ounces) frozen pineapple, thawed and drained
1 package (about 12 ounces) frozen peaches, thawed and drained
2 tablespoons kirsch
⅔ cup apricot preserves
¾ cup sliced almonds, toasted
4 bananas

1 Prepare cake mix with water, following label directions; pour batter into a 10-inch tube pan.

2 Bake in moderate oven (350°) 45 minutes, or until a long wooden skewer inserted near center comes out clean.

3 Hang cake in pan upside down over a quart-size soft drink bottle; cool completely. Loosen cake around edge and tube with a knife; invert onto a large serving plate.

4 Combine pineapple, peaches, and kirsch in a medium-size bowl; toss lightly. Chill at least an hour to blend flavors.

5 Starting ½ inch in from outer edge of cake, cut a cone-shape piece from center, using a sharp knife and a sawing motion; lift out and wrap to serve for another dessert.

6 Heat preserves just until bubbly in a small saucepan; press through a sieve into a small bowl. Brush over outside of cake to glaze evenly; press almonds into glaze.

7 Just before serving, peel bananas and slice; add to chilled fruits; spoon into hollow in cake. Garnish with maraschino cherries, if you wish. Cut cake in wedges, serving some of the fruit with each piece.

Chocolate Angel Ring

Easy, different way with angel-cake mix: Add cocoa to the batter and it's chocolate
Bake at 350° for 45 minutes. Makes one 10-inch tube

    1 package angel-cake mix
      Water
    ¼ cup sifted dry cocoa (not a mix)
    1 tablespoon instant coffee powder
    ½ cup boiling water
    1 package fluffy white frosting mix
      Flaked coconut

1 Prepare cake mix with water, following label directions. Sprinkle cocoa, alternately with 2 more tablespoons water, over batter and fold in completely; pour batter into a 10-inch tube pan.
2 Bake in moderate oven (350°) 45 minutes, or until a long wooden skewer inserted near center comes out clean.
3 Hang cake in pan upside down over a quart-size soft-drink bottle; cool completely. Loosen cake around edge and tube with a knife; invert onto a large serving plate.
4 Dissolve instant coffee in boiling water in a small deep bowl; add frosting mix. Prepare, following label directions. Spread over side and top of cake. Sprinkle generously with coconut. Cut in wedges.

Orange Sunburst

Chiffon cake, orange all around—even filling. Cake is split into layers; orange marmalade's the go-between
Makes one 10-inch tube cake

    1 package orange chiffon-cake mix
      Eggs
      Water
    ½ cup sugar
    ¼ cup light rum
    ¾ cup orange marmalade
      EASY ORANGE FROSTING (recipe follows)
    ½ cup chopped pistachio nuts
    2 seedless oranges, pared, sectioned, and
      drained

1 Prepare cake mix with eggs and water, bake in a 10-inch tube pan, cool, and remove from pan, following label directions. Split cake horizontally; lift off top layer; turn cut edge up.
2 Combine sugar and ½ cup water in a small saucepan. Heat, stirring constantly, to boiling, then simmer 2 minutes; cool slightly; stir in rum. Spoon over cake layers.

3 Spread ½ cup of the orange marmalade over bottom layer; place on a serving plate. Top with remaining layer, cut side down.
4 Prepare EASY ORANGE FROSTING; spread over side and top of cake, making deep swirls with spatula.
5 Heat remaining ¼ cup orange marmalade until melted in a small saucepan; place pistachio nuts on wax paper. Dip one end of each orange section into marmalade, then into pistachio nuts. Arrange on top of cake. Cut in wedges.
   EASY ORANGE FROSTING—In the top of a large double boiler, combine 2 unbeaten egg whites, 1¼ cups sugar, 1 tablespoon light corn syrup, and ¼ cup thawed frozen concentrate for orange juice; place top over simmering water. Cook, beating constantly with an electric beater at high speed, 10 minutes, or until frosting stands in firm peaks; remove from heat. Makes enough to frost 1 ten-inch tube cake.

Gold Coast Pineapple Cake

Bake at 350° for 30 minutes. Makes one 9-inch four-layer cake

    1 package pineapple cake mix
      Eggs
      Water
    1 jar (10 ounces) orange marmalade
    ¼ cup thawed frozen concentrate for pine-
      apple-orange juice
    2 packages fluffy white frosting mix

1 Prepare cake mix with eggs and water, bake in 2 9x1½-inch round layer-cake pans, remove from pans, and cool, following label directions. Split each layer with a sharp knife to make 4 thin layers. Spread 3 of the layers with orange marmalade; leave remaining layer plain.
2 Heat ¼ cup water and pineapple-orange concentrate to boiling in a small saucepan; combine with 1 package of the frosting mix. Beat, following label directions. Spread over marmalade-covered layers; stack back together on a serving plate; top with plain layer.
3 Prepare remaining package of frosting mix with boiling water, following label directions; spread over side and top of cake, making deep swirls with spatula. Leave plain, or decorate with halved pineapple slices, orange wedges, and candied cherries, if you wish.

Daffodil Torte

This rich four-tier beauty with its fillings of cream and preserves hides several secrets for fast fixing
Bake at 325° for 50 minutes. Makes one 10-inch tube cake

Can you believe this show-stopper is made from a mix? It is and so is its frosting; the filling is marmalade.

1 package angel-cake mix
  Yellow food coloring
1 cup (8-ounce carton) dairy sour cream
½ cup finely chopped almonds (from a 5-ounce can)
¾ cup apricot preserves (from a 12-ounce jar)
  10X (confectioners' powdered) sugar

1 Prepare angel-cake mix, following label directions; spoon half the batter into a second bowl; tint pale yellow with food coloring.
2 Spoon batters, alternating white and yellow, into a 10-inch tube pan to make a layer. Repeat with remaining batters, alternating colors, to make a second layer. (Do not stir batters in pan.)
3 Bake in slow oven (325°) 50 minutes, or until golden and top springs back when pressed with fingertip.
4 Invert pan, placing tube over a quart-size soft drink bottle; cool cake completely.
5 Loosen around edge and tube with a knife. Turn out onto a wire rack. Split into 4 even layers.
6 Mix sour cream with almonds in a small bowl.
7 Place largest cake layer on a serving plate; spread with one third of the cream-nut mixture, then ¼ cup of the apricot preserves. Repeat with remaining layers and fillings, stacking cake

back into shape. Sprinkle 10X sugar over top and side. Chill several hours, or overnight. Slice into wedges with a sharp thin-blade knife.

●

Pineapple-Pecan Crown Cake
Luscious best describes this feathery-light chiffon cake that bakes upside down
Bake at 350° for 50 minutes. Makes one 10-inch tube cake

1 package orange-chiffon cake mix
½ cup pecan halves
1 can (about 14 ounces) crushed pineapple, drained
1 cup firmly packed light brown sugar

1 Prepare cake mix, following label directions; set aside while preparing pan.
2 Butter the inside of a 10-cup tube mold or pan well; arrange pecans in a ring on bottom. Mix drained pineapple and brown sugar in small bowl; press against side of pan with spatula. (Part will slide to bottom of pan, but this will not affect baking.) Spoon batter into pan.
3 Bake in moderate oven (350°) 50 minutes, or until top is golden and springs back when pressed with fingertip.
4 Cool in pan on wire rack 15 minutes. Loosen around top and tube with spatula; turn upside down on serving plate; lift off pan.
5 Slice into wedges; serve warm.

●

Valentine Alaska
A beautiful build-up of cherry cake mix with ice cream between the layers and quick-bake meringue of fluffy frosting

Bake cake at 350° for 30 minutes and meringue at 400° for 3 minutes. Makes 6 to 8 servings plus a bonus cake layer

1 package cherry cake mix
  Egg whites
  Water
1 square pint firm vanilla ice cream
1 package fluffy white frosting mix
  Boiling water
½ cup sliced toasted almonds
¼ cup strawberry preserves

1 Prepare cake mix with egg whites and water, following label directions. Pour batter into 2 greased-and-floured baking pans, 9x9x2.
2 Bake in moderate oven (350°) 30 minutes, or until centers spring back when lightly pressed with fingertip. Cool in pans on wire racks 10 minutes; remove from pans; cool completely. Wrap one layer and set aside to frost for another meal.
3 About 15 minutes before serving, cut remaining cake square in half; place one half on a cutting board or ovenproof platter slightly larger than cake.
4 Halve square of ice cream horizontally; place pieces on cake, trimming as needed to fit. Press remaining half cake layer on top. Place in freezer while preparing frosting meringue.
5 Prepare frosting mix with boiling water, following label directions. Measure out about ½ cup if you wish to make the heart trim; spread remainder over side and top of filled cake. Shape outline of heart on top with saved frosting, building up side about ¼ inch. Press almonds into frosting along sides of cake.
6 Bake in hot oven (400°) 3 minutes, or until

The coating for Valentine Alaska is frosting mix instead of a meringue.

*Pink Apple Chiffon Cake,
a mix-based beauty with
Apple-Cranberry Filling
and a satiny cool coat of
whipped cream "icing".*

frosting is tipped with gold. Spoon preserves into heart on top; cut cake into thick slices with a sharp knife.

●

Pink Apple Chiffon Cake

Bake at 350° for 45 minutes. Makes one 10-inch tube cake

Cake:

1 package lemon chiffon cake mix
   Water
   Eggs
1 teaspoon ground mace

Apple-Cranberry Filling:

2 medium-size baking apples, pared, quartered, cored, and thinly sliced
1 can (8 ounces) whole berry cranberry sauce
2 tablespoons sugar
1 teaspoon grated orange rind
1 envelope unflavored gelatin
¼ cup water
   Few drops red food coloring
1 pint cream for whipping

1 Prepare cake mix with water and eggs, following label directions but substituting mace for lemon rind. Pour batter into an ungreased 10-inch tube pan.

2 Bake in moderate oven (350°) 45 minutes, or until top springs back when lightly pressed with fingertip.

3 Invert pan, placing tube over a quart-size soft drink bottle; let cake cool completely. Loosen cake around the edge and the tube with a spatula. Cover pan with a serving plate; turn upside down; gently lift off pan. Cut cake into 3 layers.

4 Apple-Cranberry Filling: Combine apples, cranberry sauce, sugar, and orange rind in a medium-size saucepan. Heat to boiling; reduce heat; cover. Simmer about 10 minutes, or until apples are tender.

5 Soften gelatin in water in a cup; stir into hot apple mixture. Add food coloring to tint a pretty pink. Pour into a medium-size bowl.

6 Set bowl in a larger bowl partly filled with ice and water to speed setting. Chill, stirring often, until as thick as unbeaten egg white.

7 Beat cream until stiff in a medium-size bowl. Fold 1⅓ cups into apple mixture.

467

8 Spread ⅓ of the filling between each layer; frost top with remainder. Frost and decorate side of cake with remaining whipped cream. Chill until ready to serve. Decorate with mint leaves and sugar-sprinkled fresh cranberries, if you wish.

Pecan Cream Cake

Coffee flavors the rich filling and frosting; pecans and orange, the cake
Bake at 325° for 45 minutes. Makes one 9-inch two-layer cake

1 package yellow cake mix
2 eggs
   Water
1 teaspoon orange extract
1 teaspoon almond extract
1 cup finely chopped pecans
   MOCHA CUSTARD FILLING (recipe follows)
   MOCHA CREAM FROSTING (recipe follows)

1 Blend cake mix with eggs, water, and orange and almond extracts in a large bowl; add pecans and beat, following label directions. Pour into two greased and floured 9x1½-inch round layer-cake pans.
2 Bake in slow oven (325°) 45 minutes, or until centers spring back when pressed with fingertip. Cool layers in pans on wire racks 5 minutes; turn out onto racks; cool completely.
3 Put layers together with chilled MOCHA CUSTARD FILLING; frost side and top with MOCHA CREAM FROSTING. Chill until serving time.

Mocha Custard Filling

3 tablespoons sugar
2 tablespoons flour
⅛ teaspoon instant coffee powder
½ teaspoon vanilla
⅔ cup milk, scalded
1 egg

1 Combine sugar, flour, instant coffee, and vanilla in the top of a double boiler; slowly stir in scalded milk. Cool, stirring constantly, over simmering water 3 minutes, or until mixture thickens.
2 Beat egg slightly in a small bowl, then *very slowly* beat in hot mixture; return to double boiler. Continue cooking, stirring constantly, 5 minutes, or until mixture thickens again; chill.

Mocha Cream Frosting

1 cup cream for whipping
3 tablespoons sugar
1 teaspoon instant coffee powder
½ teaspoon vanilla

Combine ingredients in a bowl; chill 30 minutes; beat until stiff.

Savannah Cake Squares

Broiled frosting is rich with peanut butter, coconut, and cream
Makes one cake, 13x9x2

1 package yellow cake mix
½ cup (1 stick) butter or margarine
1 can (3¼ ounces) flaked coconut
1 cup firmly packed light brown sugar
½ cup crunchy peanut butter
⅓ cup light cream or table cream

1 Prepare cake mix and bake in a pan, 13x9x2, following label directions.
2 While cake bakes, melt butter or margarine in a medium-size saucepan; remove from heat. Stir in remaining ingredients.
3 Remove cake from oven; turn heat to BROIL. Spread topping over hot cake.
4 Broil, 4 to 6 inches from heat, 1 minute, or just until frosting bubbles; cool. Cut in about-3-inch squares.

Almond Sparkle Cake

Bake cake from a mix, then top with a mellow hot syrup. It's different and so good!
Bake at 375° for 30 minutes. Makes one 9-inch layer

1 package loaf-size yellow cake mix
½ cup toasted slivered almonds (from a 5-ounce can)
½ cup sugar (for syrup)
½ cup water
1 tablespoon lemon juice
¼ teaspoon almond extract
1 tablespoon sugar (for topping)

1 Prepare cake mix, following label directions; stir in slivered almonds. Pour into a greased 9x1½-inch round layer-cake pan.
2 Bake in moderate oven (375°) 30 minutes, or until top springs back when lightly pressed with fingertip. Cool cake in pan on wire rack 10 minutes.
3 While cake cools, heat ½ cup sugar and water to boiling in small saucepan, then simmer 5 minutes. Stir in lemon juice and almond extract; remove from heat.

4 Turn cake out onto serving plate; pour hot syrup over slowly, letting it soak into cake. Sprinkle top with the 1 tablespoon sugar. Cut into 6 wedges; serve warm.

Shadow Cream Cake

Four thin cream-filled layers are topped with vanilla frosting and trimmed with chocolate to make this cake-mix beauty
Makes two 9-inch layers

1 package French-vanilla cake mix
1 package (about 4 ounces) vanilla-flavor pudding mix
1 cup (6-ounce package) semisweet chocolate pieces
1 package French-vanilla frosting mix
1 tablespoon vegetable shortening

1 Prepare and bake cake mix in two 9x1½-inch layer-cake pans, then cool, following label directions. Remove from pans.
2 Prepare pudding mix, following label directions; remove from heat. Stir in ½ cup of the semisweet-chocolate pieces until melted; chill. (Save remaining ½ cup chocolate for Step 5.)
3 Prepare frosting mix, following label directions.
4 Split each cake layer to make 4 thin layers. Put together with pudding filling between each; place on serving plate. Spread prepared frosting on top and side of cake.
5 Melt saved ½ cup semisweet-chocolate pieces with shortening in small saucepan over hot water; drizzle from tip of teaspoon around edge of cake, letting it drip down side.

Quick Sachertorte

Four dark layers with a double filling and chocolate frosting make this delectable beauty
Bake at 350° for 25 minutes. Makes two 9-inch layers

1 package sour-cream fudge cake mix
  Eggs
  Water
1 jar (12 ounces) apricot preserves
1 can (1 pound, 5 ounces) chocolate frosting

1 Grease two 9x1½-inch round layer-cake pans; dust lightly with flour, tapping out any excess.
2 Prepare cake mix with eggs and water, following label directions; pour into prepared pans.
3 Bake in moderate oven (350°) 25 minutes, or until tops spring back when lightly pressed

with fingertip. Cool in pans on wire racks 10 minutes; loosen around edges with a knife; turn out onto racks; cool completely.
4 When ready to put torte together, heat apricot preserves slowly in a small saucepan, stirring constantly, just until hot; press through a sieve into a small bowl; cool.
5 Split cake layers to make 4 thin layers. Spread each of 3 with ⅓ cup of the chocolate frosting, then ⅓ cup of the apricot preserves; stack back together on a serving plate. Top with plain layer.
6 Frost side and top of torte thinly with remaining chocolate frosting; chill. Cut in thin wedges, for it's rich.

Peachy Upside-Down Cake

Top, fragrantly warm, with a fluff of whipped cream or ice cream for a double-sweet treat
Bake at 350° for 50 minutes. Makes one cake, 8x8x2 plus a bonus 8-inch layer

 4 tablespoons (½ stick) butter or margarine
 ½ cup firmly packed brown sugar
 1 can (1 pound) sliced cling peaches, drained
 ½ cup toasted slivered almonds
 1 package spicecake mix

1 Melt butter or margarine in baking pan, 8x8x2; stir in brown sugar.
2 Arrange peach slices in rows on sugar mixture; sprinkle with almonds.
3 Prepare spicecake mix, following label directions; pour half of batter (about 2¾ cups) over peaches and almonds in pan. (Pour remaining batter into buttered 8x1½-inch layer-cake pan to bake in same oven for another dessert.)
4 Bake peach dessert in moderate oven (350°) 50 minutes, or until top springs back when lightly pressed with fingertip. (Bake layer 30 minutes.)
5 Cool on wire rack 5 minutes; turn out onto serving plate.
6 Cut into squares; serve warm, plain or with whipped cream, if you wish.

Rose Crown

Here's a perfect way to honor someone special on a birthday or anniversary
Bake at 375° for 30 minutes. Makes one 10-inch tube cake

1 package angel-cake mix
  Water
2 packages fluffy white frosting mix
1 pound sifted 10X (confectioners' powdered) sugar
  Green, red, and yellow food colorings

1 Prepare cake mix with water, bake in a 10-inch tube pan, cool, and remove from pan, following label directions.

2 Prepare 1 package of the frosting mix with boiling water, following label directions; stir in 10X sugar, 1 cup at a time, just until frosting is stiff enough to hold its shape. Spoon one third into a small bowl; tint green with a few drops food coloring. Stir a few drops each red and yellow food colorings into remaining to tint light orange; measure out ¼ cup and set aside for Step 7.

3 To make roses: Cut 15 small pieces of wax paper; place one on the top of a small jar, holding in place with a dot of frosting. (This makes a handy holder.)

4 Fit a flower tip onto a cake-decorating set; fill with orange frosting. Hold decorator horizontally with wide end of tip at center of wax paper, and gently and evenly press out frosting, turning jar at the same time, to make a tight center for rose. Continue pressing frosting around center in short overlapping strokes to make petals. Remove paper from jar; place on a cooky sheet. Repeat to make 15 roses in all; let stand until firm.

5 Prepare remaining package of frosting mix with boiling water, following label directions; tint pale yellow with food coloring; frost cake. Peel roses from wax paper; arrange on cake.

6 Wash cake-decorating set; fit with writing tip; fill with green frosting. Press out stems for bittersweet. Change to leaf tip; press out leaves around roses.

7 Blend a drop or two each red and yellow food colorings into saved ¼ cup orange frosting to darken; shape bittersweet berries on cake. Store cake at room temperature.

●

Daffodil Cake
Bring out your cooky press to shape the colorful posies quickly and easily
Bake at 350° for 30 minutes. Makes one cake, 13x9x2

Above, Rose Crown, a cake-mix angel cake, frosted with a mix, tinted sunny gold and strewn with roses.

Left: confectioner's masterpiece? Not at all. It's Toasted Almond Torte and you can make it yourself.

1 package white cake mix
    Eggs
    Water
1 package creamy vanilla frosting mix
4 tablespoons (½ stick) butter or margarine
3 cups sifted 10X (confectioners' powdered)
    sugar
    Green, yellow, and red food colorings
1 package fluffy white frosting mix

1 Prepare cake mix with eggs and water, bake in a pan, 13x9x2, cool, and remove from pan, following label directions.

Above, easy Daffodil Cake, made from a mix. Its garden of daffodils is fashioned from a frosting mix.

Above right, a basket of berries atop a spice cake (from a mix). Berry Blossom recipe tells you how.

2 Prepare vanilla frosting mix with butter or margarine and warm water, following label directions; divide in half.
3 Stir 1 cup of the 10X sugar into one half of the frosting; tint green with food coloring; set aside for Step 7.
4 Stir remaining 10X sugar into other half; measure 2 tablespoonfuls into a cup for making centers of blossoms; tint remaining yellow with food coloring.
5 Fit snowflake or star plate on a cooky press; fill with yellow frosting; press out onto a wax-paper-lined cooky sheet to make 6 blossoms. Shape the 2 tablespoons saved white frosting into 6 tiny balls; press one into center of each blossom, then gently make a hollow in each with a wooden spoon handle. Mix a few drops each yellow and red food colorings in a cup to make orange; lightly brush around edges of flower cups. Cover and chill until firm.
6 Prepare fluffy frosting mix with boiling water, following label directions; frost cake.
7 Fit a writing tip onto a cake-decorating set; fill with saved green frosting; press out onto cake in ribbons to divide into 12 sections. Pipe bowknots and long slender leaves, alternately, into sections. Peel chilled blossoms from wax paper; set in place on top of leaves. Store cake at room temperature until serving time.

471

Tips for Decorating Berry-Blossom Cake, Daffodil Cake, Toasted Almond Torte and Rose Crown

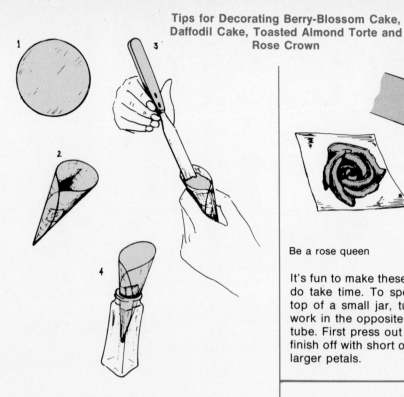

Be a rose queen

It's fun to make these showy beauties, but they do take time. To speed the job, work on the top of a small jar, turning it one way as you work in the opposite direction with decorating tube. First press out tight center of rose, then finish off with short overlapping strokes for the larger petals.

When you make candy cornucopias

Cut circles of wax paper and shape into cones for the handy molds. Spread melted chocolate inside each to cover completely, then stand upright in a small-neck bottle until chocolate hardens. This helps cone keep its rounded shape.

472

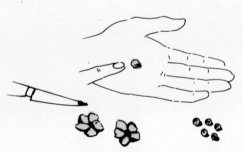

Create a whimsical extra

With imagination, you can design many fancies, such as the blossom shown on our strawberry cake. To make: Flatten tiny balls of frosting with your finger; arrange, overlapping, to form petals. For center, sieve tinted frosting, pick up on a knife point and drop into place.

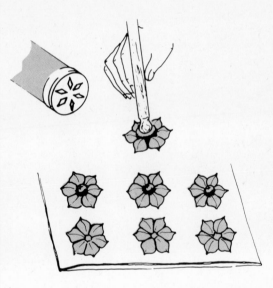

To "grow" daffodils

Force frosting through your cooky press to form the sunny blossoms. For flower cups, roll bits of soft frosting into tiny balls, place one in the center of each posy, and hollow lightly with a wooden-spoon handle.

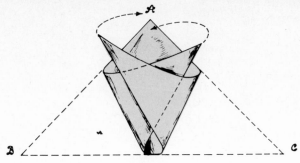

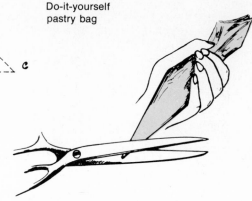

Do-it-yourself
pastry bag

No pastry bag? Make one this way: Tear off a 12-inch square of wax paper, fold it into a triangle, and cut in half. Holding corners B and C of long side, curl toward A as shown, pulling tightly until all three points meet. (Point at bottom should be closed.) Fill cone with frosting; snip off point to whatever size opening you wish.

● ● ●

Berry-Blossom Cake
With its sparkly red berry trim, it's as inviting as spring's first fresh fruit
Bake at 350° for 1 hour. Makes one deep 8-inch square cake

1 package spicecake mix
  Eggs
  Water
2 packages creamy vanilla frosting mix
½ cup (1 stick) butter or margarine
  Green and red food colorings
2 cups sifted 10X (confectioners' powdered) sugar
  Red decorating sugar

1 Grease a deep square 10-cup baking dish; flour lightly.
2 Prepare cake mix with eggs and water, following label directions; pour into prepared dish.
3 Bake in moderate oven (350°) 1 hour, or until top springs back when lightly pressed with fingertip. Cool in dish on a wire rack 10 minutes; turn out onto rack; cool completely.
4 Prepare 1 package of the frosting mix with ¼ cup of the butter or margarine and warm water, following label directions; frost cake.
5 Prepare remaining package of frosting mix with remaining butter or margarine and warm water, following label directions; measure out ½ cup and tint green with food coloring. Fit a writing tip onto a cake-decorating set; fill with

green frosting; press out onto sides of cake to form lattice trim.
6 Stir 10X sugar into remaining frosting until smooth and very stiff. Divide in half; tint one half green and the other half pink with food colorings.
7 Pinch off green frosting, ½ teaspoonful at a time, and shape into ovals; flatten each with palm of hand to make leaves; draw on markings with a wooden pick; chill until firm.
8 Pinch off pink frosting, 1 teaspoonful at a time, and shape into strawberries; roll in red sugar on waxed paper to coat well; chill.
9 Arrange strawberries, tip ends up, on top of cake; tuck leaves between strawberries. Chill cake until serving time.

●

Toasted Almond Butter Torte
Candylike chocolate cones create such a big effect for so little effort
Bake at 350° for 35 minutes. Makes two 9-inch layers

½ cup semisweet-chocolate pieces
1 package yellow cake mix
  Eggs
  Water
1 package (6 ounces) sliced almonds
1 package creamy fudge frosting mix
½ cup (1 stick) butter or margarine
1 tablespoon instant coffee powder

473

1 package creamy vanilla frosting mix
1½ cups sifted 10X (confectioners' powdered) sugar

1 Cut six 3-inch rounds from wax paper; shape each into a cone; fasten with cellophane tape.
2 Melt chocolate pieces in the top of a double boiler over simmering water; cool, then spread thinly inside paper cones to cover completely. Stand each upright in a small bottle; chill until firm.
3 Prepare cake mix with eggs and water, bake in two 9x1½-inch layer-cake pans, cool, and remove from pans, following label directions.
4 While cake bakes, spread almonds in a shallow pan; heat in same oven 12 minutes, or until lightly toasted; set aside.
5 Prepare fudge frosting mix with ¼ cup of the butter or margarine and warm water, following label directions.
6 Dissolve instant coffee in ¼ cup warm water in a medium-size bowl; add vanilla frosting mix and remaining ¼ cup butter or margarine; prepare, following label directions; stir in 10X sugar until smooth. Measure out 1 cup and set aside for next step. Put cake layers together with remaining coffee frosting. Place on a serving plate. Spread chocolate frosting on side and top of cake; sprinkle all over with toasted almonds.
7 Fit a fancy tube onto a cake-decorating set; fill with saved 1 cup coffee frosting; press into chocolate cones to fill. Carefully peel papers from cones; arrange on top of cake. Press remaining coffee frosting in rosettes around bottom of cake. Chill until serving time.

Strawberry Cream Squares
Bake at 350° for 20 minutes. Makes about 3 dozen

1 package lemon cake mix
  Eggs
  Water
1 teaspoon almond extract
1 package strawberry-flavor whipped-dessert mix
  Milk
1½ cups strawberries, washed, hulled, and sliced thin
1 cup cream for whipping

1 Grease two baking pans, 15x10x1; line bottoms with wax paper; grease paper. (If you have only one pan, bake half of the batter at a time, keeping remainder chilled.)
2 Prepare cake mix with eggs and water, following label directions; stir in almond extract. Pour half of the batter into each pan.

3 Bake in moderate oven (350°) 20 minutes, or until centers spring back when lightly pressed with fingertip. Cool in pans on wire racks 5 minutes. Loosen around edges with a knife; invert onto racks; peel off wax paper; cool cakes completely.
4 Prepare whipped-dessert mix with milk and water, following label directions; fold in 1 cup strawberries.
5 Place 1 cake layer on a large cooky sheet or tray; spread strawberry mixture over top; cover with remaining cake layer. Chill at least an hour, or until filling is set.
6 Just before serving, beat cream until stiff in a medium-size bowl.
7 Cut cake crosswise into eighths and lengthwise into fifths; spoon a dollop of cream on top of each piece; garnish with remaining strawberry slices.

Cherry Crown Pudding
Versatile loaf-size cake mix is the beginning of this mellow rich steamed pudding
Makes 6 servings

8 maraschino cherries, well drained
1 package loaf-size yellow cake mix
¼ cup chopped pecans
¼ teaspoon ground mace
  10X (confectioners' powdered) sugar

1 Arrange cherries in bottom of a well-greased 4-cup tube mold to form a pretty pattern.
2 Prepare cake mix, following label directions; fold in pecans and mace. Pour over cherries.
3 Cover mold with foil, transparent wrap, or double thickness of wax paper; fasten with string to hold tightly.
4 Place on rack or trivet in kettle or steamer; pour in boiling water to half the depth of pudding in mold; cover tight.
5 Steam 1½ hours, or until a long thin metal skewer inserted near center comes out clean. (Keep water boiling gently during entire cooking time, adding more boiling water, if needed.)
6 Cool mold 5 minutes; loosen pudding around edge with knife; unmold onto serving plate; sprinkle with 10X sugar. Brush cherry topping with honey or white corn syrup to give it extra sparkle, if you wish.
7 Cut pudding into wedges; serve warm with whipped cream, lemon sherbet, or vanilla ice cream, if you wish.

Golden Pudding-Puff
Presto! Chiffon-cake mix bakes sky-high like a soufflé. And see how easy it is to make
Bake at 350° for 1½ hours. Makes 8 servings

More cake-mix sleight-of-hand (l. to r.): Cherry Crown Pudding, Golden Pudding-Puff and Jonquil Ribbon Cake.

1 package lemon chiffon cake mix
1½ cups water
¼ teaspoon ground ginger
1 tablespoon rum extract or flavoring
2 teaspoons vanilla
4 eggs
    Sugar
SUN-GOLD CREAM (recipe follows)

1 Prepare an 8-cup straight-side baking dish this way: Fold a piece of foil, long enough to go around dish and overlap slightly, in half lengthwise. Coat foil and dish with softened butter or margarine, then dust evenly with sugar. Wrap foil around dish, buttered side in, to make a 3-inch stand-up collar; hold in place with a paper clip and string.

2 Prepare packet of egg-white mix from chiffon cake mix package, following label directions. (Set aside for Step 4.)

3 Combine flour mixture from second packet with water in a medium-size saucepan. Cook, stirring all the time, until mixture is very thick. Remove from heat; stir in ginger, rum extract or flavoring, and vanilla.

4 Beat eggs until very thick and light in a large bowl with electric mixer at high speed. Beat cooked mixture in saucepan until very smooth with same beater. Blend slowly into beaten eggs, then fold into beaten egg-white mixture from Step 2 until no streaks of yellow or white remain.

5 Pour into prepared baking dish. Cut a deep circle in batter with knife 1 inch in from edge so dessert will puff up sky-high; sprinkle top lightly with sugar.

6 Set baking dish in a shallow pan; place on oven shelf; pour boiling water into pan to a depth of 1 inch.

7 Bake in moderate oven (350°) 1½ hours, or until puffy-light and firm in center. Remove from pan of water; cut away string and gently pull away foil collar.

8 Spoon at once into serving dishes; top with SUN-GOLD CREAM.

Sun-Gold Cream

Fluffy, tart, and spicy, it goes pleasingly with the airy-light pudding-puff
Makes about 2 cups

½ cup sugar
1 teaspoon all-purpose flour
¼ teaspoon ground ginger
¼ teaspoon salt
2 eggs
½ cup orange juice
⅓ cup lemon juice
¼ cup cream for whipping

1 Mix sugar, flour, ginger, and salt in a cup.

2 Beat eggs slightly in top of a small double boiler; blend in dry ingredients, then stir in orange and lemon juices.

3 Cook, stirring constantly, over simmering water, 5 minutes, or until mixture coats a metal spoon; remove from heat. Strain into a medium-size bowl; cover; chill.

4 Just before serving, beat cream until stiff in a small bowl; fold into chilled mixture.

Jonquil Ribbon Cake

Here's sleight-of-hand baking. Middle layer looks like a big pinwheel before cake is put together. Step 7 tells the secret
Bake at 375° for 15 minutes for oblong cake, 20 minutes for layers. Makes three 9-inch layers

1 package sponge cake mix
1 jar (1 pound) peach jam
1 tablespoon 10X (confectioners' powdered) sugar
1 package creamy vanilla-frosting mix

1 Grease bottom of baking pan, 15x10x1; line with wax paper cut ½ inch smaller than pan; grease paper. Grease bottoms of two 9x1½-inch layer-cake pans; line with wax paper; grease paper.

2 Prepare sponge cake mix, following label directions. Measure 4 cups batter into prepared jelly-roll pan, spreading evenly into corners; divide remaining batter evenly into layer-cake pans.

3 Bake in moderate oven (375°) 15 minutes for oblong cake, 20 minutes for layers, or until tops spring back when lightly pressed with fingertip. (Cake in oblong pan is to be rolled, so watch carefully that it doesn't bake too dry.)

4 While cakes bake, press jam through a sieve or purée in an electric blender, ready for spreading in Step 7.

5 As soon as oblong cake is done, loosen around sides of pan with knife; invert onto a clean towel dusted with 10X sugar; peel off wax paper. Roll up; let cool 10 minutes.

6 When layers are done, cool in pans on wire rack 5 minutes; loosen around edges with knife; invert onto racks. Peel off wax paper; cool layers completely.

7 Unroll oblong cake; spread with half of jam, then cut lengthwise into 8 strips, each 1¼ inches wide. (Measure with a ruler so strips will be even.) Save remaining half of jam for Step 9.

8 Roll up 1 strip, jelly-roll fashion; lay flat on a cooky sheet. Matching ends, wind remaining strips, 1 at a time, around roll to make a big pinwheel about 9 inches in diameter; chill at least 30 minutes.

9 Put cake together this way: Place one layer, top side down, on a serving plate; spread with part of the saved jam; top with the chilled cake roll, lifting it carefully with a pancake turner. Spread remaining jam on flat side (bottom) of second layer; place, jam side down, on cake roll to make 3 layers.

10 Prepare frosting mix, following label directions. Frost side, then top of cake, making peaks all over with tip of teaspoon.

11 Chill until serving time. Slice into wedges with a sharp knife.

Golden Fruit Cake

Bake at 325° for 1 hour and 40 minutes. Makes one 10-inch tube cake

  2 packages pound-cake mix
  4 eggs
    Milk or water
  1 jar (8 ounces) candied red cherries, chopped
  1 cup whole blanched almonds, chopped
  ½ cup golden raisins, chopped
  ¼ cup cognac
  1 can (3½ ounces) flaked coconut
  2 tablespoons grated orange rind
  1 tablespoon grated lemon rind
    Orange Frosting (recipe follows)

1 Grease a 10-inch tube pan; flour lightly, tapping out any excess.

2 Prepare both packages of pound-cake mix with eggs and milk or water, following label directions.

3 Combine cherries, almonds, and raisins in a medium-size bowl; stir in cognac. Fold into batter with coconut and orange and lemon rinds. Spoon into prepared pan.

4 Bake in slow oven (325°) 1 hour and 40 minutes, or until top springs back when lightly pressed with fingertip. Cool 10 minutes in pan on a wire rack. Loosen cake around edge and tube with a knife; turn out onto rack; turn right side up; cool completely.

5 Wrap cake in wax paper or transparent wrap, then in heavy foil; freeze up to 8 weeks.

6 The day before serving, remove cake from freezer; let stand, still wrapped, at room temperature to thaw. Several hours before serving, unwrap cake; place on a serving plate.

7 Make ORANGE FROSTING: spread over top of cake, letting mixture run down side. Decorate with cut candied red cherries, angelica, and whole almonds, if you wish.

Orange Frosting

Combine 1½ cups sifted 10X (confectioners' powdered) sugar, 1 tablespoon cognac, and 1 tablespoon orange juice in a small bowl; beat until smooth.

Note: If serving cake without freezing, wrap and store in the refrigerator for at least a week to mellow, then frost.

Easter Bunny Cake

Base is a round layer; pictures show how to cut and shape

To make 1 bunny cake, you'll need:
  1 package loaf-size yellow cake mix
  1 package white frosting mix
  ¼ cup strawberry jam
  ¾ cup canned flaked coconut
    Marshmallows and pink gumdrops

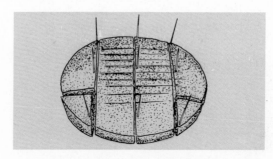

Prepare and bake cake mix, following label directions for one 9x1½-inch layer; cool; remove from pan. Cut into 4 two-inch-wide strips, then cut a piece about 2 inches long from one end of each outside strip. (Wooden picks make handy cutting guidelines.) Make frosting; fold ½ cup into jam.

Put each two cake pieces of same size together with jam filling. Place, cut sides down, on wax-paper-lined tray, as shown. Frost all over; sprinkle with coconut. Use marshmallows for tail, gumdrops for eyes, nose. Cut ears from bottom of envelopes; unfold and poke into frosting.

477

CANDY KITCHEN:
ALL ABOUT SWEETENERS, COOK'S
GUIDE TO CHOCOLATE, TEMPERATURES
AND TESTS, OLD FASHIONED
CANDIES, NO-COOK CANDIES

How many women were introduced to cooking via candy? By beating a pan of fudge, impatient for the rich chocolate mixture "to turn," lose its gloss, become candy? By pulling golden strands of taffy while they were still too hot to hold, even with buttery fingers? By licking a spoon drifted with snowy divinity?

A great many, no doubt, because family candy-making sessions are among a child's earliest memories. And certainly among his fondest.

Candy-making, alas, is becoming a lost art. Too many excellent commercial candies on the market. Too many calorie-conscious people. Too bad, because there is the same sort of involvement in making candy that there is in baking yeast bread. Candies, like yeast doughs, must be worked with the hands—kneaded, pulled, shaped, decorated. And the satisfaction that comes of making silky fudge or cloud-light divinity is equally as great as that derived from baking a tall perfect loaf of bread. Try some of the recipes that follow—you'll see. And involve the whole family in the candy-making. You'll be glad you did. And so will they.

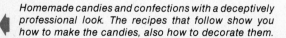

Homemade candies and confections with a deceptively professional look. The recipes that follow show you how to make the candies, also how to decorate them.

ALL ABOUT SUGARS AND SWEETENERS

Sugar—a barrel of choices
Granulated—Take your pick of cane or beet sugars, in bag or box, for both are excellent and our cheapest energy food. Watch for specials on 5- or 10-pound bags, for they are the thriftiest buys of all. Other products in this class are super-fine or very fine sugar often called for in special cake, pudding, and candy recipes; tablets and cubes in various sizes and shapes in 1-, 1½-, and 2-pound cartons; cinnamon-sugar, ready to sprinkle right from the jar on breakfast toast or a fruit dessert; and a variety of colored sugars for decorating cookies, cakes, and candies. Compared to granulated sugar, all of the specialty items cost more, but are often worth it in convenience.
10X—Also known as confectioners' or confectioners' powdered, this is our popular frosting sugar and is labeled both 10X and 4X. The X's simply mean a slight difference in texture, with 10X being the finer of the two.
Brown—This favorite owes its color and flavor to the small amount of molasses that clings to the sugar crystals during processing. You'll find it labeled LIGHT, MEDIUM, or DARK BROWN, in 1-pound cartons, or, in some areas, in 2-pound transparent bags. Which you choose depends on your flavor preference. Consider, too, GRAN-

479

ULATED BROWN SUGAR, packed in 1-pound, 4-ounce cartons. As its name suggests, it pours easily and does not need to be packed before measuring.

Syrups—a world of variety

Corn and Cane—Their names identify their source, and there are both light and dark kinds. Some are a pure syrup; others have sugar and flavoring added.

Blended—Look around, for there's a choice to suit every taste, and true to their name, they are a blend of several pure syrups. Those labeled pancake or waffle syrup combine corn and cane syrups; butter-blended has butter added; and flavored syrups mix maple, fruit, or honey flavors with the syrup. Babies of the family are fruit-juice syrups that are cooked with sugar to pour over pancakes or desserts.

Maple—Famous for its delicate flavor, it comes from the sap of the maple tree. And since it takes about 45 gallons of sap to produce a gallon of pure syrup, it carries a de luxe price tag. Other items to consider are maple-sugar syrup, maple-blended syrup, and flavored maple syrup.

Honey—The flavor and color depend upon the kinds of flowers from which the bees gather nectar. Most usual: Clover or alfalfa. Color is your best guide to flavor, for light honey is mild, while dark tastes stronger. Along with liquid honey in glass jars, pails, and squeeze tubes, you'll find comb honey in 4-inch-square wooden frames, chunk or bulk honey, and granulated or crystalline honey, often labeled CREAMED.

480

Molasses—Depending on how it is made, it may be either sulphured or unsulphured, but both are equally good. Blackstrap molasses, a result of the final boiling in sugar-making, has a black color and strong flavor. Although sometimes promoted as a health food, it has the same food value as regular molasses.

The right way to store sugars and syrups

Granulated, very fine, and 10X sugars—Store all in a very dry place or in a tightly covered container to keep out moisture and prevent lumping. If granulated sugar should harden into a cake, try these first-aid tricks: Cover it, set in a warm place to dry out, then crush in a blender or roll with a rolling pin. If it turns very hard, it's easiest to make it into a sugar-water syrup to use for sweetening beverages or fruits. At times you may find your supply getting ahead of you, but it's good practice to buy often and only what you can use within two or three weeks.

Brown sugar—It needs moisture, so your refrigerator is a perfect keeper. Or, empty the package into a transparent bag and seal tightly; it will stay soft for many weeks. Some cooks place a slice of bread or a cut piece of apple in the canister, and these, too, help to keep the sugar moist. If it cakes, simply put it in a paper bag, wrap the bag in a damp cloth, and let it stand until soft.

Syrups—Your cupboard shelf is the best storage spot. Wipe the neck of the bottle or jar with a damp cloth after each use, and recap lightly. This lets in just enough air to prevent mold and crystallization. The exceptions are fruit syrups, which usually need chilling. Check the label to make sure.

Maple syrup—Once opened, it should be kept in the refrigerator. If mold appears, no harm done. Just skim it off, and heat the syrup to boiling. Or if it forms a crust on top, heat until the sugar dissolves.

Honey—To preserve its fresh flavor and aroma, keep the jar tightly covered in a dry place, for chilling gives it a cloudy look. If it gets sugary and thick, simply heat honey in its jar in lukewarm water until honey is syrupy.

How does sugar measure up?

If you're fixing a special recipe, it pays to know just how much sugar to buy. Here is a pin-up guide for quick reference:

- One pound of granulated sugar measures 2⅓ cups.
- One pound 10X (confectioners' powdered) sugar yields 4 cups if unsifted, or about 4½ cups if sifted.
- One pound light or dark brown sugar, firmly packed, measures 2¼ to 2⅓ cups.
- One pound of loaf sugar—120 pieces.

How would the confectioner manage without chocolate? For making fudge, dipping fondants and fruit centers?

COOK'S GUIDE TO CHOCOLATE

Each kind of chocolate has its own personality; for best results, use the type specified in your recipe. To new cooks and old hands: Here are get-acquainted and brush-up notes on buying, storing, melting

CHOICES IN CHOCOLATE

Unsweetened—Often referred to as baking or cooking chocolate, this old-timer in the bar-shape package has a rich bitter flavor that's ideal for brownies, cookies, fudge, cakes, sauces, desserts. Each package, weighing 8 ounces, contains separately wrapped 1-ounce squares.

Liquid unsweetened—Pack in 1-ounce transparent envelopes, this needs no melting or measuring, can be squeezed handily right from the envelope into batter or beverage. Use it in any recipe that calls for unsweetened chocolate or cocoa, 1 envelope for 1 square of chocolate or ¼ cup dry cocoa.

Semisweet—It looks like unsweetened bar chocolate and is packaged the same way, but it contains some sugar. It melts smoothly and quickly to stir into frostings, fillings, and candies.

Semisweet pieces—Unsweetened chocolate plus cocoa butter, sugar, and a vanilla-type flavoring go into this popular ingredient. Although the tiny nuggets will melt creamy-smooth for candy or sauces, they hold their shape during baking in cakes and cookies. Package sizes: Six and 12 ounces.

Sweet—Also tagged sweet-cooking chocolate, each 4-ounce bar contains 18 small squares of a special blend: Unsweetened chocolate, sugar, cocoa butter, and vanilla. For cakes, pies, frostings, and sauces that need a rich but light flavor, it's an excellent choice. Although not a milk chocolate, it's a delicious stand-in for a candy bar.

Milk chocolate—The popular candy-bar chocolate, made somewhat like sweet chocolate but with cream added to give it a lighter color and milder flavor. Buy it in bars, bulk, or pieces to suit your preference.

Today's candy counters are a happy hunting ground, with their almost unlimited variety of solid milk-chocolate bars, chocolate-coated candy, and dozens of combination bars containing fruits and nuts alone or together. You've

481

probably noticed, too, that many of your favorite recipes call for a chocolate bar to add interesting flavor and crunch. And when it comes to timesavers, most cooks will agree that a melted chocolate bar is a mighty fast way to a frosting.

Cocoa—This breakfast regular is unsweetened chocolate with most of the cocoa butter (fat) removed. "Dutch process" marked on the label simply tells you that the cocoa has been treated to give it a rich dark color and robust flavor. Expect to pay a little bit more for this type than for regular cocoa.

Instant cocoa *mixes,* not to be confused with regular cocoa, are a blend of cocoa, sugar, flavoring, and sometimes nonfat dry milk. Stir them into hot or cold milk or water for an instant pickup. Container sizes vary from 8 ounces to 2 pounds. Reminder: In recipes—for baked foods and candies, especially—*do not substitute instant cocoa mix for cocoa.*

STORAGE HOW-TO'S

With chocolate as with most foods, there's a best method of storing. Basically, it should be kept cool—about 75°—and dry. If chocolate gets warmer, the cocoa butter comes to the surface, melts, and forms a grayish white film as it cools. While this doesn't affect the flavor, it does mar the appearance. Sometimes, under the best conditions, this happens anyway. If it does, just melt the chocolate—this restores its color.

Chocolate may also be kept in the refrigerator, provided you wrap it first, then place in a tightly covered container so it won't absorb odors. Keep cocoa in a tightly sealed container in a cool spot (not the refrigerator). Under other conditions it, too, fades and tends to lump.

HOW TO MELT CHOCOLATE

Methods are many, but one precaution is a must with them all: Go easy on the heat—chocolate burns and scorches quickly. Unsweetened, semisweet, and sweet may be melted over hot (*not boiling*) water, but guard against moisture or steam; either causes the chocolate to stiffen.

Another trick is to place the chocolate in a greased pie plate in a warm oven until melted. Unsweetened chocolate may also be melted in a heavy saucepan over very low direct heat, but this takes constant watching and stirring. For

some recipes, such as candies, double up on steps by melting the chocolate with the butter or margarine, or in the liquid (milk, water, or coffee).

A favorite of many homemakers that's practically effortless: Place the chocolate in a double boiler over water; cover; heat until water bubbles, then turn off the heat. Let stand until chocolate softens; stir until smooth.

TOPPERS AND TRIMS

Cakes, pies, cookies, candies, puddings, and ice-cream desserts take on a professional look with a garnish of grated chocolate or chocolate curls. To grate: Start with cold chocolate, a dry

cold grater, and cold hands. Rub the square up and down over the grating surface, working quickly and handling the chocolate as little as possible.

To make curls: Warm a square of chocolate slightly at room temperature, then, for little

curls, shave thin strips from the narrow side with a vegetable parer; for large ones, from the bottom. Pick up the curls with a wooden pick (otherwise they shatter) and chill until firm before arranging on food.

Fabulous Fudge

To be a topnotch fudge maker, it pays to invest in a candy thermometer to eliminate guesswork. The rest is easy—just follow mixing-cooking directions
Makes about 1¼ pounds

2 cups sugar
⅛ teaspoon salt
2 squares unsweetened chocolate
1 small can evaporated milk (⅔ cup)
2 tablespoons white corn syrup
2 tablespoons butter or margarine
½ teaspoon vanilla

1 Combine sugar, salt, chocolate, evaporated milk, and corn syrup in a heavy saucepan. Heat, stirring constantly, just until the sugar dissolves and chocolate melts. Remove spoon; put thermometer in.

2 Cook rapidly, without stirring, to 236°, remove from heat. Add butter or margarine and vanilla (no stirring yet), then let cool on a wire rack to 110°. Bottom of the pan should feel lukewarm.

3 Beat 2 to 3 minutes, or until fudge starts to thicken and lose its glossiness; pour into buttered dish, 10x6x2. Let stand until set—only 2 to 3 minutes; cut at once in smooth neat squares.

●

Creamy Cocoa Fudge
Candy fans love this old-fashioned treat
Makes 1¼ pounds

⅓ *cup dry cocoa* (not a mix)
2 *cups sugar*

Dash of salt
⅔ *cup water*
2 *tablespoons butter or margarine*
1 *teaspoon vanilla*

1 Combine cocoa, sugar, salt, water, and butter or margarine in a medium-size saucepan. Heat slowly, stirring constantly, to boiling, then cook, without stirring, to 236° on a candy thermometer. (A teaspoon of syrup dropped into cold water will form a soft ball.) Remove from heat; stir in vanilla.

2 Set pan aside on kitchen counter (not in refrigerator) and let cool, *without stirring,* to 110° on candy thermometer. (Bottom of pan should feel lukewarm.)

3 Beat mixture 2 to 3 minutes, or just until it starts to thicken and loses its glossiness.

4 Spoon at once, into 10 one-ounce paper cups or souffle cups or into a buttered loaf pan, 7½x3¾x2¼. (Candy will be about 1-inch deep in loaf pan.)

5 Let stand at room temperature until firm.

TEMPERATURES AND TESTS FOR CANDY

Type of Candy	Temperature on Candy Thermometer (at Sea Level) Degrees F.	Test	Description of Test
Sugar Suryp	230 to 234	Thread	Syrup spins a 2-inch thread when dropped from fork or spoon.
Fondant, Fudge	234 to 240	Soft Ball	Syrup, when dropped into very cold water, forms a soft ball that flattens on removal from water.
Caramels	244 to 248	Firm Ball	Syrup, when dropped into very cold water, forms a firm ball that does not flatten on removal from water.
Divinity, Marshmallows	250 to 266	Hard ball	Syrup, when dropped into very cold water, forms a ball that is hard enough to hold its shape, yet still plastic.
Taffy	270 to 290	Soft Crack	Syrup, when dropped into very cold water, separates into threads that are hard but not brittle.
Brittle, Glacé	300 to 310	Hard Crack	Syrup, when dropped into very cold water, separates into threads that are hard and brittle.

483

Chocolate Truffle Fudge
Makes about 2 pounds

1 can (14 or 15 ounces) sweetened condensed milk
2 packages (12 ounces each) semisweet-chocolate pieces
Pinch of salt
2 teaspoons vanilla
1 cup finely chopped walnuts

1 Combine sweetened condensed milk, semi-sweet-chocolate pieces, and salt in top of double boiler; heat over simmering water, stirring often, 10 to 12 minutes, or until chocolate is melted. Remove from heat; stir in vanilla, then fold in ¾ cup walnuts.
2 Spread evenly in a buttered 8-inch foil pie plate or in a wax-paper-lined pan, 8x8x2. Sprinkle remaining ¼ cup walnuts over, pressing into fudge. Chill 3 hours, or until firm.

Frosted Penuche Squares
Like penuche and divinity? They're doubly good when combined in one treat
Makes 2 pounds

Basic Penuche
2 cups firmly packed brown sugar
1½ cups granulated sugar
3 tablespoons butter or margarine
¼ teaspoon salt
1½ cups milk

Basic Divinity
2 cups sugar
½ cup light corn syrup
½ cup water
2 egg whites
1 teaspoon vanilla
½ cup chopped pistachio nuts

484

1 Make Basic Penuche: Combine brown and granulated sugars, butter or margarine, salt, and milk in a large heavy saucepan.
2 Heat, stirring constantly, just until sugar dissolves, then cook rapidly, without stirring, to 240° on a candy thermometer. (A teaspoonful of syrup will form a soft ball when dropped into cold water.) Remove from heat.
3 Cool in pan on a wire rack to 110°, or until bottom of pan feels lukewarm.
4 Beat 8 to 10 minutes, or until mixture is light in color and very thick. (It will still be glossy.) Pour into a buttered pan, 8x8x2; cool.
5 Make Basic Divinity: Combine sugar, corn

syrup, and water in a medium-size heavy saucepan. Heat, stirring constantly, to boiling. (Have a fork wrapped in a piece of damp cheesecloth handy and wipe off any sugar crystals that form on side of pan as mixture heats.)
6 Cook rapidly, without stirring, to 260° on a candy thermometer. (A teaspoonful of syrup will form a hard ball when dropped in cold water.) Remove from heat.
7 While syrup cooks, beat egg whites until they stand in firm peaks in a medium-size bowl. *Beating constantly,* pour in syrup in a fine stream; beat in vanilla, then continue beating until mixture is very stiff and holds its shape. Spread over butterscotch layer in pan. Sprinkle with pistachio nuts.
8 Let stand until firm. Cut in small squares.

Caramel-Pecan Fudge Rounds
Shape this buttery-rich chocolate confection into rolls to slice as needed
Makes about 2½ pounds

2 cups sugar
⅛ teaspoon salt
2 squares unsweetened chocolate
1 small can evaporated milk (⅔ cup)
2 tablespoons light corn syrup
2 tablespoons butter or margarine
1 teaspoon vanilla
1 package (14 ounces) caramels
1 tablespoon water
2 cups coarsely broken pecans

1 Combine sugar, salt, chocolate, evaporated milk, and corn syrup in a large heavy saucepan.
2 Heat, stirring constantly, just until sugar dissolves and chocolate melts, then cook rapidly, without stirring, to 236° on a candy thermometer. (A teaspoonful of syrup will form a soft ball when dropped in cold water.) Remove from heat.
3 Add butter or margarine and vanilla. (Do not stir in.) Let cool in pan on a wire rack to 110°, or until bottom of pan feels lukewarm.
4 Beat 2 to 3 minutes, or just until fudge starts to thicken and lose its glossiness; pour onto a buttered platter. Let stand 2 to 3 minutes, or just until set and cool enough to handle.
5 Pick up fudge, about half at a time, in your hands and knead until soft. Shape each half into two rolls about 1 inch in diameter and 6 inches long. Place on wax paper.
6 Unwrap caramels and combine with water in the top of a double boiler; heat over hot water, stirring several times, until melted and mixture is creamy-smooth; cool slightly.
7 Spread pecans on a large sheet of wax paper. Working with one fudge roll at a time, spread

about half lengthwise with caramel mixture; roll in pecans to coat well. Turn roll; spread remaining with caramel mixture; roll in pecans. Repeat with remaining fudge rolls. Let stand until coating is firm.

8 Wrap rolls tightly in wax paper, foil, or transparent wrap. Store in refrigerator. When ready to serve, slice about ½ inch thick.

Golden Fudge

So satiny-smooth and creamy it literally melts in your mouth
Makes about 1½ pounds

3 cups sugar
¼ cup light corn syrup
3 tablespoons butter or margarine
½ teaspoon salt
1 cup evaporated milk
½ cup water
2 teaspoons vanilla
   Green and red candied cherries

1 Combine sugar, corn syrup, butter or margarine, salt, evaporated milk, and water in a medium-size heavy saucepan.
2 Heat, stirring constantly, to boiling, then cook rapidly, stirring several times, to 238° on a candy thermometer. (A teaspoonful of syrup will form a soft ball when dropped in cold water.) Remove from heat at once. Add vanilla, but do not stir in.
3 Cool mixture in pan to 110°, or until lukewarm; beat 2 to 3 minutes, or until it starts to thicken and lose its gloss.
4 Spread in a buttered pan, 8x8x2. Let stand 2 to 3 minutes, or just until set; cut into squares. Decorate each with slivered cherries. Let stand until firm.

Basic White Fondant

Makes about 1½ pounds

3 cups sifted granulated sugar
1 cup hot water
1 tablespoon white corn syrup
   OR: ⅛ teaspoon cream of tartar

1 Combine ingredients; cook together until candy thermometer reads 238°-242°.

2 Pour mixture onto marble slab or stainless steel pan until it cools to 110°.
3 Work syrup until it is thick, white, and creamy. Cool, then shape into balls for dipping in melted chocolate or knead in a few drops red, yellow or green food coloring and shape in fondant molds.

Shaped Fondants

Rubber fondant molds are available from bakery and confectioners' supply houses or by mail from The Maid of Scandinavia Co., 3245 Raleigh Avenue, Minneapolis, Minn. 55416. Sprinkle molds with confectioners' sugar. Place a piece of white or colored fondant in a basin over a pan of hot water; heat just until soft and pliable. Press fondant into molds. Trim edges. Leave to firm at room temperature 1 to 1½ hours. Turn molded fondants out onto a sheet of wax paper and leave for another 1 to 1½ hours.

Cherry Puffs

Tinted coconut and candied fruit top each of these wispy sweet morsels
Makes about 1¼ pounds

1 cup flaked coconut
   Red and green food colorings
2 cups sugar
½ cup light corn syrup
½ cup water
2 egg whites
1 teaspoon vanilla
   Candied red cherries, halved
   Candied green cherries, halved

1 Place ½ cup of the coconut, a drop or two red food coloring, and a drop or two water in a jar with a tight-fitting lid; shake until coconut is evenly tinted. Repeat with remaining coconut and green food coloring. Set aside for Step 5.
2 Combine sugar, corn syrup, and water in a medium-size heavy saucepan; heat, stirring constantly, to boiling. (Have a fork wrapped in a piece of damp cheesecloth handy and wipe off any sugar crystals that form on side of pan as mixture heats.)
3 Cook rapidly, without stirring, to 260° on a candy thermometer. (A teaspoonful of syrup will form a hard ball when dropped in cold water.) Remove pan from heat.
4 While syrup cooks, beat egg whites until they stand in firm peaks in a medium-size bowl. *Beating constantly,* pour in syrup in a fine stream; beat in vanilla, then continue beating

485

until mixture is very stiff and holds its shape. Stir in a few drops red food coloring to tint pale pink.

5 Drop mixture by teaspoonfuls into small mounds onto foil- or wax-paper-lined cooky sheets. Top half with pink coconut and red candied cherries, and remaining with green coconut and green cherries. Let candies stand until firm.

Butter Cream Centers
Makes about 1½ pounds, enough for 40 candies

3 cups sugar
1 cup water
¼ teaspoon cream of tartar
¼ cup butter
¼ teaspoon salt
1 teaspoon vanilla
⅛ teaspoon baking soda in ½ teaspoon hot water

1 Cook sugar, water, and cream of tartar to 238°-240° on a candy thermometer. Add baking soda and hot water, mixed, to the combination.
2 Pour onto cool marble or a stainless steel pan. Let stand 5 minutes, or until center feels lukewarm (110-115° on a candy thermometer).
3 Cream 5 minutes; add butter; work like fondant until cool and thick, 10 minutes. Knead 1 minute. Add nuts or other flavorings. Cool, then shape into balls for dipping in melted chocolate.

Chocolate for Dipping
Note: 1 pound of chocolate makes 1½ cups when melted or enough to cover 2 to 2½ pounds of centers. It is advisable to use dipping chocolate or coating chocolate. For every pound of melted chocolate, add 1 teaspoon of vanilla extract.
To melt: Shred or cut chocolate in small pieces; place in upper part of double boiler, with the water underneath at 175° on a candy thermometer. Add one pound first, then, if needed, second and third pounds as each melts down. Keep pot covered and stir chocolate after first 10 minutes. Remove from heat; cover, let stand over hot water an additional 10 minutes. Then remove from hot water, and beat until completely melted. After 1 minute, check temperature; if original chocolate was coarse and grainy melt to 120°; if medium, 110°, if extremely fine, 100°?
To condition chocolate for dipping: Let it cool to 70° (stirring occasionally until temperature drops to 80°).

When chocolate turns plastic and thick (like custard) when dropped from a spoon, place it in top part of double boiler, over water that's 115°, for 1 to 2 minutes. After 1 minute, stir chocolate as quickly as possible and remove from water. With thermometer in center, allow to cool until temperature levels off to about 90°. If temperature levels off below 90°, recondition.

To test if chocolate is right for dipping, dip several centers using a two-pronged dipping fork and twirling tail end of chocolate into a curlicue on top of each candy. Chocolate should set within five minutes to a glossy finish.

Divinity-Nut Puffs
These wisps of creamy candy are a delight at holidaytime. One batch makes two kinds
Makes about 1½ pounds

2 cups sugar
½ cup light corn syrup
½ cup water
2 egg whites
½ teaspoon lemon extract
½ teaspoon almond extract
  Few drops green food coloring
24 blanched almonds (from an about-5-ounce can)
2 tablespoons chopped pistachio nuts

1 Combine sugar, corn syrup, and water in a medium-size saucepan; heat, stirring several times, to boiling. (Have a fork wrapped in a piece of damp cheesecloth handy and wipe off any sugar crystals that form on side of pan as mixture heats.)
2 Cook rapidly, without stirring, to 240° on a candy thermometer. (A teaspoon of syrup dropped into cold water will form a soft ball that flattens very slightly.)
3 While syrup cooks, beat egg whites until they stand in firm peaks in the medium-size bowl of an electric mixer. Beating constantly, pour ⅓ of the syrup over egg whites in a fine stream to form a meringue.
4 Cook remaining syrup rapidly to 265° on candy thermometer. (A teaspoon of syrup dropped into cold water will form a ball that is hard enough to hold its shape.)
5 Pour, still beating constantly, in a fine stream over meringue mixture; continue beating until mixture is very stiff and holds its shape.
6 Divide into two bowls. Stir lemon extract into one bowl and almond extract and several drops green food coloring into second bowl.
7 Drop by teaspoonfuls into small mounds on wax-paper-lined or foil-lined cooky sheets. Top

each white mound with an almond (toast first, if you wish); sprinkle each green mound with pistachio nuts. (If candy turns too stiff while shaping mounds, beat in one or two *drops* hot water.) Let stand until firm.

Note—Choose a clear dry day to make this candy. When air is damp or humid, meringue mixture may pick up moisture, causing puffs to flatten and become sticky. Make not more than three or four days ahead, then store between layers of wax paper, foil, or transparent wrap in a container with a tight-fitting cover to keep out moisture.

Full Cream Caramels
Makes about 1½ pounds

  2 *cups sugar*
  1 *cup light corn syrup*
1½ *cups warm cream for whipping with ½ cup water*
  ¼ *cup butter*
  ½ *teaspoon salt*
  1 *teaspoon vanilla*

1 Cook sugar, syrup, 1 cup cream and ¼ cup water for 10 minutes. Add remaining warm cream and remaining water; cook slowly for 5 minutes.
2 Add butter, small amount at a time. When candy thermometer reaches 230°, lower heat; cook slowly to 244-246° on thermometer.
3 Allow to stand 10 minutes. Add salt, vanilla and pour into well-oiled or buttered 18-inch pan. Cool until solid enough to cut, then, if you like, dip into chocolate.

Fruit Caramels
Good keepers and travelers, they're an ideal choice for a gift box
Makes about 2½ pounds

  ¾ *cup golden raisins*
  ¼ *cup dried apricot halves*
1¼ *cups firmly packed brown sugar*
1¼ *cups light corn syrup*
1⅔ *cups light cream or table cream*
  ¾ *teaspoon salt*
1½ *teaspoons rum flavoring or extract*

1 Chop raisins and apricot halves very fine. Set aside for Step 3.
2 Combine brown sugar, corn syrup, cream, and salt in a medium-size heavy saucepan. Heat

Divinity-Nut Puffs, tinted delicate colors, are so dainty and light they magically melt in your mouth.

slowly, stirring constantly, to boiling, then cook rapidly, stirring constantly, to 246° on a candy thermometer. (A teaspoonful of syrup will form a firm ball when dropped in cold water.) Remove from heat at once.

3 Stir in chopped fruits and rum flavoring or extract. Pour into a buttered pan, 8x8x2. Chill just until firm.

4 Loosen candy around edges with a knife; invert onto a cutting board; cut into 1-inch squares.

●

Pralines

Buttery-rich and packed with pecans, this version boasts a quick-fix trick
Makes about 2 pounds

1 package (3 ounces) vanilla-flavor pudding
  and pie filling mix
1½ cups firmly packed light brown sugar
½ cup evaporated milk
1 tablespoon butter or margarine
2 cups pecan halves

1 Combine pudding mix, brown sugar, evaporated milk, and butter or margarine in a medium-size heavy saucepan. Heat slowly, stirring constantly, until sugar dissolves, then cook, without stirring, to 238° on a candy thermometer. (A teaspoonful of syrup will form a soft ball when dropped in cold water.) Remove from heat at once.

2 Stir in pecans, then beat with a wooden spoon 2 to 3 minutes, or until mixture starts to thicken.

3 Drop by tablespoonfuls, 2 inches apart, on wax paper. (If mixture hardens as you work, set pan over hot water.) Let stand until firm.

●

Coconut Clusters

Each little drop tastes like butterscotch fudge laced with plenty of coconut
Makes about 1½ pounds

1½ cups firmly packed brown sugar
¼ cup granulated sugar
¼ teaspoon ground cinnamon
½ cup water
2 tablespoons butter or margarine
½ teaspoon vanilla
1 can (about 4 ounces) flaked coconut

1 Combine brown and granulated sugars, cinnamon, and water in a medium-size heavy saucepan. Heat slowly, stirring constantly, until

◀ *A sparkly brittle, ready to break in small pieces.*

sugars dissolve, then cook rapidly, without stirring, to 238° on a candy thermometer. (A teaspoonful of syrup will form a soft ball when dropped in cold water.) Remove from heat at once.

2 Stir in butter or margarine. Cool mixture in pan on a wire rack to 200°. Stir in vanilla and coconut, then beat several minutes, or until mixture holds its shape but is still glossy.

3 Drop by teaspoonfuls, 1 inch apart, on wax paper. Let stand until firm.

Butter-Nut Brittle

Baking soda makes this candy puffy-light and shattery-crisp. A good keeper, it can be made weeks ahead of the holiday rush
Makes about 2 pounds

2 cups sugar
1 cup light corn syrup
1 cup water
3 cups dry toasted mixed nuts (from 2 about-
  9-ounce jars)
  OR: 3 cups unsalted roasted mixed nuts
2 tablespoons butter or margarine
2 teaspoons vanilla
2 teaspoons baking soda

1 Butter a baking pan, 15x10x1.

2 Mix sugar, corn syrup, and water in a large *heavy* saucepan; cover; heat to boiling. Uncover and cook rapidly to 236° on a candy thermometer. (A teaspoon of syrup dropped into cold water will form a soft ball.)

3 Stir in nuts slowly, keeping mixture bubbling all the time, then cook rapidly, stirring constantly, to 280° on candy thermometer. (A teaspoon of syrup dropped in cold water will form a very hard ball.)

4 Stir in butter or margarine; continue cooking to 300° on candy thermometer. (A teaspoon of syrup dropped into cold water will separate into threads that are hard and brittle.) Remove from heat.

5 Stir in vanilla; sprinkle soda over top quickly, then stir vigorously about 15 seconds, or until mixture is puffy.

6 Pour into prepared pan at once; cool completely. Break into bite-size pieces. Store in a container that has a tight-fitting lid.

●

Molasses Taffy

Ask your young cooks to join you in an old-fashioned taffy pull
Makes about 1½ pounds

489

2 cups sugar
3 tablespoons butter or margarine
¼ teaspoon salt
½ cup molasses
½ cup water
2 teaspoons cider vinegar

1 Combine all ingredients in a large heavy saucepan.
2 Heat, stirring constantly, until sugar dissolves, then cook rapidly, without stirring, to 265° on a candy thermometer. (A teaspoonful of syrup will form a hard ball when dropped in cold water.) Remove from heat.
3 Pour onto a buttered large platter; cool until easy to handle.
4 Butter hands generously. Pick up candy, half at a time, and pull back and forth until golden and candy holds its shape. (Tip: While working with part of the candy, place remaining in a barely warm oven [200°] to keep soft.) Twist each half into a rope about 1 inch in diameter. Snip into 1-inch lengths with scissors. Let stand on waxed paper until firm.
5 Wrap each piece in wax paper, foil, or transparent wrap, twisting ends to seal. Store in a cool, dry place.

Choco-Caramel Top Hats
Almost like magic, packaged caramels turn into the richest sweet-tooth tempter
Makes about 2 pounds

1 package (14 ounces) caramels
¼ cup cream for whipping
1 can (8 ounces) walnuts (2 cups)
6 squares semisweet chocolate

1 Unwrap caramels and combine with cream in the top of a medium-size double boiler. Heat over simmering water about an hour; stir until creamy-smooth. Break walnuts coarsely and stir in.
2 Drop by teaspoonfuls, 1 inch apart, on buttered cooky sheets. Let stand at least an hour, or until firm.
3 While caramel mixture cools, wash top of double boiler, then heat semisweet chocolate over hot water until partly melted; remove from heat; stir until completely melted.
4 Drop, ¼ teaspoonful for each, onto top of caramels; spread slightly. Let stand until firm.

Caramel Popcorn Balls
Makes ten 4-inch balls

⅔ cup sugar
⅔ cup light corn syrup
½ teaspoon salt
8 cups popped corn
25 caramel candy cubes

1 Combine sugar, corn syrup, and salt in a small saucepan. Heat, stirring, until sugar dissolves.
2 Pour over 8 cups popped corn in a kettle; toss to coat evenly. Cook slowly, stirring, 5 minutes more, or until very sticky.
3 Shape about ¾ cup at a time into a ball; stick a straw into each; repeat to make 10 balls.
4 Melt caramel cubes in double boiler over simmering water; spread with small spatula over top of balls; set on a buttered pan to cool and harden. Wrap in transparent wrap, if you like.

Popcorn Balls
Makes 16 to 24

⅔ cup sugar
⅔ cup light corn syrup
½ teaspoon salt
8 cups popped corn

1 Combine sugar, corn syrup, and salt in a saucepan. Heat, stirring, until sugar dissolves; remove from heat.
2 Pour over 8 cups popped corn in a kettle; toss to coat evenly. Cook slowly, stirring, 5 minutes more, or until very sticky.
3 Shape by heaping tablespoonfuls into balls.

Tutti-Frutti Popcorn Balls
Makes about 50 small balls

10 cups freshly popped corn
1 can (6 ounces) pecans
1 jar (4 ounces) candied red cherries, halved
1 package (1 pound) 10X (confectioners' powdered) sugar, sifted
⅔ cup light corn syrup
2 tablespoons water
Red food coloring
16 large marshmallows (¼ pound)
¾ teaspoon peppermint extract

1 Mix popcorn, pecans, and cherries in two buttered jelly-roll pans.
2 Combine about 1 cup of the 10X sugar, corn syrup, and water in a medium-size saucepan. Heat slowly, stirring constantly, until sugar dis-

490

solves; stir in a few drops food coloring to tint light pink.

3 Stir in remaining 10X sugar slowly; heat, stirring constantly, to boiling. Stir in marshmallows until melted; remove from heat. Stir in peppermint extract.

4 Pour half of the syrup over popcorn mixture in each pan; toss until evenly coated. Cool until easy to handle, then shape into 1½-inch balls. Let stand on wax paper until firm. Store in a tightly covered container.

Almond-Popcorn Clusters
Makes about 2½ dozen

⅓ cup sugar
3 tablespoons molasses
3 tablespoons dark corn syrup
1 teaspoon butter or margarine
1 teaspoon lemon juice
4 cups freshly popped corn
1 package (6 ounces) whole unblanched almonds (about 1 cup)
1 cup salted toasted coconut chips (from a 4-ounce can)

1 Combine sugar, molasses, corn syrup, butter or margarine, and lemon juice in a kettle. Heat slowly, stirring constantly, just until sugar dissolves; remove from heat.

2 Stir in popcorn, almonds, and coconut chips; toss until evenly coated. Cook, stirring constantly, over medium heat, 5 minutes, or until mixture is very sticky.

3 Spoon out onto wax paper. Let stand a few minutes until cool enough to handle, then shape into 2-inch clusters. Let stand until coating is firm and dry. Store in a loosely covered container.

Pralines, Butter-Nut Brittle and a light fudge with nuts added, all gaily wrapped. Lucky the recipient!

Turkish Mint Jelly Candies
Makes about 1 pound

¾ cup granulated sugar
⅔ cup water
5 tablespoons plus ⅓ cup cornstarch
1⅓ cups 10X (confectioners' powdered) sugar
1 cup water
⅛ teaspoon cream of tartar
¼ teaspoon peppermint oil
green food coloring

1 Grease a 9x5x3-inch loaf pan. Line with wax paper.
2 Place granulated sugar and ⅔ cup water in a heavy 1½-quart pan. Stir over gentle heat until sugar has dissolved, about 3 to 4 minutes. Attach sugar thermometer to pan. Increase heat and bring to boil. Boil without stirring for 7 to 10 minutes, until sugar thermometer registers 240° or a drop of syrup forms a soft ball when dropped into cold water.
3 Meanwhile, mix 5 tablespoons cornstarch with 1 cup 10X sugar and 1 cup water. Stir until boiling (paste will be clear and thick). When the sugar reaches the desired temperature, quickly stir in cream of tartar and pour all at once into the cornstarch mixture. Stir well until smooth, then simmer for 10 minutes over medium heat, stirring constantly. Remove pan from heat. Flavor with peppermint oil and add a few drops green food coloring. Pour into prepared loaf pan. Leave to set unrefrigerated for 12 hours.
4 For coating the candies, sift ⅓ cup 10X sugar and ⅓ cup cornstarch onto a board. Loosen sides of jelled candy in pan and turn out onto board. Cut into 4 strips lengthwise. Cut each strip into 8 pieces. Coat each piece with sugar and cornstarch mixture. Store in box, sprinkling sugar and cornstarch between each layer. Candy will keep for about 4 weeks in an airtight container.

Basic Marshmallows
Makes about 1½ pounds

2 cups sifted sugar
¾ cup hot water
1 cup light corn syrup
1½ teaspoons vanilla or other flavoring
2½ tablespoons unflavored gelatin softened in
¾ cup cold water

1 In large pan, combine sugar, hot water, ½ cup syrup. Blend well; cook over high heat until candy thermometer reads 240°.
2 Turn off heat, add ½ cup corn syrup. Add softened gelatin to syrup. Stir gently.
3 Pour at once into an 8″ ovenproof glass bowl.

Immediately begin beating it, accelerating speed. Beat hard for 10 minutes, or until mixture is lukewarm, snowy white, and heavy.
4 Add flavoring.
5 Pour into 7″ pans greased with vegetable shortening. Store 8 hours. Cover with 10X (confectioners' powdered) sugar, and cut with greased knife. Roll pieces in 10X sugar to cover well.

Jolly Jellies
These sparkly gems take fussing, but just one batch makes three flavors
Makes about 2½ pounds

3 cups sugar
4 envelopes unflavored gelatin
⅛ teaspoon salt
2½ cups water
Lemon extract and oils of peppermint and anise
Yellow, green, and red food colorings

1 Mix sugar, gelatin, and salt in a large saucepan; stir in water. Heat, stirring often, to boiling; simmer 15 minutes; remove from heat.
2 Pour 1½ cups into a pan, 7x4x2; stir in ½ teaspoon lemon extract and a few drops yellow food coloring. Pour 1 cup of remaining mixture into each of two other pans. Stir 2 drops oil of peppermint and green food coloring into one pan and 2 drops oil of anise and red food coloring into remaining. Let all stand at room temperature overnight, or until firm. (To make fancy shapes, pour part of each mixture into 1-inch cooky molds.)
3 Loosen gelatin in each pan around edges; pull out onto cutting board sprinkled with sugar. Cut in small squares; roll in sugar.

Candied Fruit Peel
This sweet treat is different. Freshly made, it's tangy and soft and stays just that way. Plain gelatin dissolved in the syrupy coating is the secret. Because it's such a good keeper, it can be made up early for gifts, family snacks, or a garnish for holiday fruit salads and desserts.
Makes 1½ pounds

Peel from 3 oranges
Peel from 1 grapefruit
2½ cups sugar

What fun! Candied Apples made by dipping shining red apples in a syrup made of red-hot cinnamon candies.

1 tablespoon light corn syrup
1 teaspoon ground ginger
⅛ teaspoon salt
1½ cups water
1 envelope unflavored gelatin

Follow these easy steps:
1 Peel rind from fruits in quarters; trim off white membrane, then cut rind into ¼-inch-wide strips. Place in large saucepan with water to cover; heat to boiling; simmer 15 minutes. Drain; repeat cooking with fresh water and draining two more times. Return rind to pan.
2 Stir in 2 cups of the sugar, corn syrup, ginger, salt, and 1 cup of the water. Cook slowly, stirring often from bottom of pan, 40 minutes, or until most of syrup is absorbed. Have the gelatin softened in remaining ½ cup water ready; stir it in until dissolved, then cool.
3 Lift out strips, one at a time, and roll in remaining ½ cup sugar, sprinkled on a sheet of wax paper, to coat generously. Place in a single layer on a cooky sheet to dry slightly. If stored in a tightly covered container, peel will keep fragrantly moist for weeks.

Candied Apples
Makes 8

8 medium-size red apples
8 flat wooden skewers
2 cups sugar
1 cup light corn syrup
½ cup water
¼ cup (1¾-ounce bottle) red cinnamon candies
10 drops red food coloring (optional)

493

1 Wash and dry apples; remove stems and insert skewers into stem ends.
2 Mix sugar, corn syrup and water in heavy 2-quart saucepan. Cook over medium heat, stirring constantly, until mixture boils and sugar is dissolved. Then cook, without stirring, until temperature reaches 250° or until small amount of syrup dropped into very cold water forms a ball which is hard enough to hold its shape, yet plastic. Add cinnamon candies and continue cooking to 285° or until small amount of syrup dropped into very cold water separates into threads which are hard, but not brittle.

3 Remove from heat. Stir in red food coloring, if desired. Hold each apple by its skewer and quickly twirl in syrup, tilting pan to cover apple with syrup. Remove apple from syrup; allow excess to drip off, then twirl to spread syrup smoothly over apple. Place on lightly greased baking sheet to cool. Store in cool place.
Note: If candy mixture cools too quickly it may be reheated over low heat.

Candied Orange Peel
Makes about 2 pounds

5 large oranges
2 cups sugar
1 cup water
3 tablespoons light corn syrup
2 packages (3 ounces each) orange-flavor gelatin

1 Cut rind of each orange in quarters with a sharp knife, then peel off. Place in a heavy large saucepan.
2 Pour in cold water to cover; heat to boiling. Simmer 10 minutes; drain. Add fresh water; simmer 5 minutes; drain.
3 Carefully scrape white membrane from rind with the tip of a teaspoon; cut rind into thin even strips.
4 Combine sugar, water, and corn syrup in same saucepan; heat over medium heat, stirring constantly, until sugar dissolves. Stir in orange rind. Cook over medium heat, stirring often from bottom of pan, 30 minutes, or until rind is almost transparent and syrup is absorbed; drain.
5 Sprinkle gelatin in a large shallow pan; roll strips while warm, one at a time, in gelatin to coat generously. Place on wire racks; let stand until dry. Store in a loosely covered container.

494

NO-COOK CANDIES

Basic Marzipan
Makes about 3½ pounds

1 pound almond paste
⅓ cup light corn syrup
1¼ cups liquid marshmallow
6 cups 10X (confectioners' powdered) sugar
    Liquid food coloring
    Whole cloves and other spices

1 Combine almond paste, corn syrup and the marshmallow in bowl. Knead ingredients to mix thoroughly. Turn out on cutting board or other smooth, flat surface. Add sugar, 1 cup at a time, working it into mixture completely each time.
2 Divide marzipan into as many colors as you choose. (Dye with liquid food coloring). Knead coloring into marzipan to blend completely.
3 Form fruits, vegetables or decorations for the tops of chocolates; sprinkle the working surface with cornstarch if candy sticks when making delicate pieces.
4 Wiping hands occasionally with damp cloth will give figures a soft shine. To obtain a brilliant shine on finished pieces, paint them with light corn syrup (diluted with hot water, if necessary).
5 Use cloves and other spices, as well as bits of contrasting pieces of marzipan for details.

Anise Drops
One batch makes two colors to decorate to suit your fancy
Makes about 1 pound

1 package (1 pound) 10X (confectioners' powdered) sugar
3 tablespoons light corn syrup
3 tablespoons water
½ teaspoon anise extract
    Red or green food coloring
    Red, green, and white decorating frostings in pressurized cans or plastic tubes

1 Combine 10X sugar, corn syrup, and water in the top of a double boiler. Heat over simmering water, stirring several times, until sugar dissolves and mixture is smooth.
2 Remove from heat, but let mixture stand over hot water to keep soft for shaping. Stir in anise extract.
3 To make white candies, drop half of mixture, a teaspoonful at a time, onto wax paper to form 1-inch rounds. Let stand until firm.
4 To tint candies, stir a few drops of either red or green food coloring into remaining mixture in top of double boiler, then shape, following directions in Step 3. Let stand until firm.
5 Decorate each with a dainty leaf or flower design, using frostings from pressurized cans.

Raisin Bonbons
Makes about 1 pound

½ cup seedless raisins
8 tablespoons peanut butter
1 tablespoon butter, softened
½ cup 10X (confectioners' powdered) sugar

Better than a commercial candy kitchen, this line-up of showy sugarplum treats that you can make yourself.

1 package (6 ounces) semisweet-chocolate pieces

1 Line a baking sheet with wax paper. Chop raisins.
2 Place peanut butter, butter, and 10X sugar in a bowl and mix until smooth. Stir in raisins.
3 Shape into balls about ½'' in diameter. Leave in a cool place until firm.
4 Place chocolate pieces in a medium-size bowl over hot, not boiling, water and leave until melted. Stir gently.
5 Dip raisin balls in the chocolate, remove with a fork, drain, and place on wax paper. Let stand until firm. Store in an airtight container.

Marzipan Vegetable Bouquet
Makes about 2 pounds

2 cans (8 ounces each) almond paste

1 jar (about 7 ounces) marshmallow cream
¼ cup light corn syrup
3¾ cups sifted 10X (confectioners' powdered) sugar
Yellow, red, green, and blue food colorings

1 Crumble almond paste into a medium-size bowl; blend in marshmallow cream and corn syrup. Stir in enough of the 10X sugar to make a very stiff dough.
2 Sprinkle remaining 10X sugar on a pastry board; turn out almond mixture into sugar. Knead 5 to 6 minutes, or until smooth and sugar is worked in completely.
3 Pinch off mixture, about a half teaspoonful at a time, and shape between palms of hands into carrots, peas in pods, radishes, yellow squash, eggplant, and potatoes, or other vegetables of your choice. Let stand on wax paper for several hours, or until dry.
4 When ready to decorate, mix small amounts of food colorings with equal parts of water in

495

custard cups. Brush lightly over "vegetables" to tint. Let stand again until dry. Store in refrigerator.

Almond Truffles
Makes about 40

6 squares (1 ounce each) semi-sweet chocolate
2 tablespoons light cream
6 ounces (⅔ cup) almond paste* or marzipan
¼ teaspoon almond extract
    for decoration: chocolate or cocoa powder; flaked coconut; chopped almonds; chocolate or multicolored sprinkles

1 Melt chocolate in top of double boiler (or in mixing bowl) over hot, not boiling, water. When completely melted, remove from heat and stir in cream, marzipan or almond paste, and almond extract. Stir until well mixed. Set 3 tablespoons of each decoration on wax paper.
2 Make small balls of candy by rolling the mixture between palms of your hands, using a heaping half-teaspoon for each ball. Roll at once in decorations.
3 Refrigerate truffles until firm, about 2 hours. Store in cool place or in refrigerator.
*Note: As an alternative, grind 1 cup blanched almonds as fine as possible in electric blender. Add to melted chocolate with additional 1 tablespoon of light cream and 1 cup 10X confectioners' sugar.

Fudge Ribbons
Candylike butterscotch and chocolate pieces are your ready-to-go secrets
Makes about 1 pound

1 package (6 ounces) butterscotch-flavor pieces
⅔ cup sweetened condensed milk (from a 14- or 15-ounce can)
2 teaspoons vanilla
1 package (6 ounces) semisweet-chocolate pieces
1 teaspoon instant coffee

1 Melt butterscotch-flavor pieces in the top of a double boiler over simmering water; remove from heat.
2 Stir in ⅓ cup of the sweetened condensed milk (not evaporated) and 1 teaspoon of the vanilla. Spread evenly into a well-buttered pan, 9x9x2, to make a thin layer.
3 Wash double-boiler top and melt semi-sweet-chocolate pieces the same way; remove from heat. Stir in remaining ⅓ cup sweetened

condensed milk, 1 teaspoon vanilla, and instant coffee. Spread evenly into a second well-buttered pan, 9x9x2. Chill layers several hours, or until firm.
4 Cut each into 6 strips, 1½ inches wide; stack three each butterscotch and chocolate strips, alternately, to make 2 six-layer bars; wrap each tightly in foil. Chill several hours, or overnight.
5 Cut each bar into 24 thin slices with a sharp knife.
Note: To store, keep bars wrapped and chilled, ready to slice just before serving.

Quick-as-a-Wink Fudge
Prepare 1 package fudge frosting mix, following label directions for fudge; stir in ½ cup chopped walnuts. Spread evenly in a buttered 8-inch foil pie plate or in a wax-paper-lined pan, 8x8x2. Sprinkle ¼ cup chopped walnuts over. Makes about three dozen pieces.

Fondant Bonbons
Young cooks will be tickled to help shape and trim these no-cook fancies
Makes about 1½ pounds

4 tablespoons (½ stick) butter or margarine
¼ cup light corn syrup
⅛ teaspoon salt
3½ cups sifted 10X (confectioners' powdered) sugar

1 Cream butter or margarine until soft in a medium-size bowl; stir in corn syrup and salt, then 10X sugar until completely blended. Knead a few minutes, or until smooth.
2 Divide mixture into four bowls; flavor, shape, and decorate, following directions below.

Chocolate Creams
Add 1 tablespoon dry cocoa powder (not a mix) and ¼ teaspoon vanilla to fondant in one bowl; knead in until completely blended. Divide into 24 even pieces; flatten each to a 1½-inch thin round on a cooky sheet. Decorate with chocolate sprinkles or colored decorating sugars of your choice. Chill until firm.

Orange Patties
Add ¼ teaspoon orange extract and a drop each red and yellow food colorings to fondant in one bowl; knead in until completely blended. Divide into 24 even pieces; flatten each to a 1½-inch thin round on a cooky sheet. Decorate with chocolate sprinkles or colored decorating sugars of your choice. Chill until firm.

Sunshine Meltaways

Add ¼ teaspoon lemon extract and a drop or two yellow food coloring to fondant in one bowl; knead in until completely blended. Divide into 24 even pieces; flatten each to a 1½-inch thin round on a cooky sheet. Decorate with red cinnamon-candy hearts or semisweet-chocolate pieces. Chill until firm.

Snowdrops

Add ¼ teaspoon vanilla to fondant in one bowl; knead in until completely blended. Divide into 24 even pieces; flatten each to a 1½-inch thin round on a cooky sheet. Decorate with red cinnamon-candy hearts, slivered red or green candied cherries, walnuts or pecans, or colored decorating sugars of your choice. Chill until firm.

Butterscotch Nougats

They taste so creamy smooth and rich with a now-and-then bite of cherries and nuts
Makes about 2 pounds

- 1 package (6 ounces) butterscotch-flavor pieces
- 1 small can evaporated milk (⅔ cup)
- 2½ cups sifted 10X (confectioners' powdered) sugar
- ½ cup chopped pistachio nuts
- ¼ cup red candied cherries (from a 4-ounce jar), chopped
- 1 can (about 4 ounces) flaked coconut

1 Combine butterscotch-flavor pieces and evaporated milk in a medium-size saucepan; heat, stirring constantly, just until butterscotch pieces melt.
2 Stir in 10X sugar, nuts, and cherries. Chill about an hour, or until firm enough to handle.
3 Shape, a rounded teaspoonful at a time, into small balls; roll in coconut on wax paper. Chill several hours, or until firm.
Note: To store, layer candies with wax paper or transparent wrap between in a tightly covered container. Keep in a cool place.

Caramel-Pecan Rounds

Almost like magic, store-bought caramels turn into luscious homemade treats
Makes about 1¼ pounds

- 1 package (14 ounces) caramels
- 2 tablespoons butter or margarine

- 1 teaspoon vanilla
- ¾ cup coarsely chopped pecans

1 Unwrap caramels and melt in the top of a double boiler over simmering water; remove melted caramel mixture from heat. Stir in butter or margarine and vanilla.
2 Pour onto a buttered platter; roll on platter with buttered hands into a log about 10 inches long.
3 Sprinkle pecans on wax paper; roll candy in nuts to coat evenly. Continue rolling as candy cools so it will keep its shape.
4 Wrap tightly in wax paper, then in foil. Let stand until firm.
5 Cut into ¼-inch-thick slices with a sharp knife.
Note: To store, keep wrapped log chilled. When ready to slice, remove from refrigerator and let stand at room temperature 30 minutes to soften.

Marshmellow Popcorn Balls

They're as easy as melting marshmallows and popping corn. Youngsters will be tickled to help with the shaping
Makes 16

- 32 large marshmallows (from an about-10-ounce package)
- 4 tablespoons (½ stick) butter or margarine
  Green food coloring
- 4 cups unsalted freshly popped popcorn

1 Combine marshmallows and butter or margarine in the top of a double boiler; heat, stirring often, over simmering water 15 minutes, or until marshmallows melt. Stir in a few drops food coloring to tint light green.
2 Pour over popcorn in a large bowl; toss with a wooden spoon until evenly coated.
3 Divide into 16 even mounds on wax paper. Butter hands lightly and shape into balls.
4 Trim with slivered red candied cherries and silver candies, if you wish. Place on wire racks until firm.
Note: To store, layer with wax paper or transparent wrap between in a shallow pan; cover.

Choco-Almond Triangles

Semisweet chocolate "frosts" a rich coconut-almond layer for these sweet-tooth tempters
Makes 72 triangles

- 1½ cups toasted slivered almonds (from two 5-ounce cans)

497

1 can (about 4 ounces) flaked coconut
2 tablespoons butter or margarine, melted
1 package (1 pound) sifted 10X (confectioners' powdered) sugar
⅓ cup evaporated milk
3 squares semisweet chocolate

1 Chop 1 cup of the almonds. (Set remaining ½ cup aside for decorating triangles in Step 4.)
2 Combine chopped almonds with coconut and melted butter or margarine in a medium-size bowl; blend in 10X sugar, alternately with evaporated milk, until well-mixed. Spoon into a buttered pan, 9x9x2, pressing down firmly with back of spoon to make an even layer.
3 Melt semisweet chocolate in a small bowl over simmering water; spread over coconut layer. Chill at least 30 minutes, or until chocolate is firm.
4 Cut lengthwise, then crosswise into sixths to make 36 squares; remove from pan. Cut each square in half diagonally. Gently press a slivered almond in top of each. Chill again.
NOTE—To store, place in a single layer in a shallow pan; cover with transparent wrap or foil and keep chilled so chocolate will stay firm.

Gumdrop Whimsies
Simple shaping tricks are what count here

BASIC DIRECTIONS—Spread about ¼ cup granulated sugar at a time onto a pastry board. With a rolling pin, roll out medium-size gumdrops in sugar, turning several times to keep them from sticking, then shape, following directions below. Let candies stand on a wire rack until slightly dry and firm enough to hold shape.
CALICO ROLLS—To make each, roll out 1 gumdrop to a 2-inch round. Cut about 6 small pieces from different-color gumdrops and arrange in a round layer; place rolled-out gumdrop on top. Roll all again into a bigger flat round, then roll up, jelly-roll fashion.
RAINBOW TRIANGLES—To make each, roll out 2 each red, yellow, and green gumdrops to a 2-inch round. Brush each round lightly with a pastry brush dipped in water; stack rounds, alternating colors. Let stand several hours to dry, then cut in quarters.
WHIRLIGIGS—To make each, roll out 2 contrasting-color gumdrops to 3-inch rounds. Place one on top of the other; fold in half, then roll into a cone shape.
ROSES—To make each, roll out a gumdrop to a 3-inch round; cut in half. Roll up one half, crimping cut edge tightly with finger to make

base of flower and flaring out top edge into petals. Roll remaining half around first half the same way, pressing together tightly at base and shaping into petals to make a full, open rose. Roll out a green gumdrop to a 2-inch round; cut out leaf shapes; press onto base of rose. Place, base down, on a wire rack to dry. Snip two small strips from a contrasting-color gumdrop and tuck into center of rose.
Note: To store, layer with wax paper or transparent wrap between in a shallow pan; cover; store in a cool place.

Apricot Creams
Dried fruits make the nicest bite-size sweets—like little no-cook candies
Makes about 1½ pounds

½ cup golden raisins
½ cup toasted slivered almonds
1 cup 10X (confectioners' powdered) sugar
2 tablespoons dairy sour cream
1 package (11 ounces) dried apricot halves

1 Chop raisins and almonds; blend with 10X sugar and sour cream in a small bowl.
2 Separate apricot halves; spoon a scant teaspoonful raisin mixture in center of each half. Chill.

Stuffed Dates
With pineapple and brown sugar in filling, an inspired sweet
Makes about 1½ pounds

1 can (about 9 ounces) crushed pineapple
1 cup oven-toasted rice cereal, crushed
2 tablespoons brown sugar
1 teaspoon grated orange rind
1 package (8 ounces) pitted dates
Granulated sugar

1 Drain syrup from pineapple. (Save to add to a fruit cup.) Blend pineapple, cereal, brown sugar, and orange rind in a small bowl.
2 Make a slit in side of each date; spread slits slightly to open; fill each with a rounded teaspoonful pineapple mixture. Roll in granulated sugar on wax paper to coat well. Store in a tightly covered container.

HOMEMADE CANDIES How to store, how to pack

Store these ways:

Fudge—Leave candy right in its pan and cover tightly with foil to keep it creamy-soft, then place it in a cool, dry spot. While fudge mellows upon standing, it's a good idea to make it no longer than a week or two ahead of serving or giving.

Caramels—To hold these chewy treats at their best, wrap each piece separately in transparent wrap so the candy shows through invitingly, and tuck away in a covered container in your cupboard.

Uncooked fondant—For top flavor, this confection should "ripen" for a few days before eating. Bundle the rolls into a plastic bag, seal tightly, and chill to slice as needed. Leaving the rolls whole helps to keep them moist and flavorful.

Pack candies for mailing like this:

Choose varieties that travel well—fudge, caramels, or fruit drops. Use a metal container and place a layer of crushed wax paper in bottom, then cut dividers of cardboard and fit into the box to help keep the pieces from shifting about.

After arranging candies attractively in their gift box, add lid and tape or tie shut for extra protection. Set container in a strong, larger carton and fill in the spaces with unsalted popped corn or crushed paper to cushion the bounce.

Wrap outer carton in heavy brown paper, tie securely, affix label (printed or typed) on one side only, and mark the package "Keep from heat." Plan to mail gifts by December 1, and remember to include ZIP Code for speedier delivery.

499

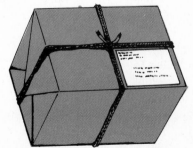

CANNY WAYS WITH

CANNED FOODS

CANNY WAYS WITH CANNED FOODS: TIPS ON BUYING, CAN WEIGHTS AND MEASURES, HOW TO STORE CANNED FOODS, QUICK TRICKS, CANNED MEATS GIVE YOUR BUDGET A BOOST, MEALTIME MAGIC

Counting all the choices, there are more than 1,300 different canned foods, from abalone to zucchini, to help you speed meal preparation, give a dish a new twist, keep your food budget down. All of this variety and service costs less than you may think, for even though most prices have risen over the last 15 years, canned foods' prices have stayed remarkably steady. To save even more, consider these good buymanship tips.

● ● ●

WAYS TO BE A CANNY BUYER

1. *Buy by brand name.* This is your assurance of quality. Labels list helpful information such as can size or weight of contents, cup measure or number of servings—often recipe and nutrition notes. When you find a brand specially suited to your need, jot down the name and can size on your recipe for easy reference the next time you shop for it.

Canned foods, every cook's shortcuts to good eating.

2. *Buy to suit your use.* Choose one quality for the table, another for cooking. Thrifty-priced canned tomatoes are perfect for soup or sauce, while the firm whole variety is better for serving as a winter vegetable or salad. If you have children in your family, consider small-size fruits in lighter syrups and cut-up vegetables. They not only taste as good, but seem to please small-fry appetites.

3. *Buy in several sizes.* Pick larger cans for table serving, smaller ones for cooking. For example: If a recipe calls for 1 cup fruit cocktail, it is thriftier to use all of a small can than part of a large one with too little left for another time.

4. *Buy at sales*. This is the ideal time to stock up on staples such as evaporated milk, fruit and vegetables, juices, and tuna. Sales like "5 for $1" save money, specially if the foods are ones you use often. Sometimes supermarkets feature "mix-and-match" sales with a variety of one canned item. For example—navy, pinto, lima, black-eye, and kidney beans. Choose all of one kind, or mix them up, as you please.

5. *Buy a few dress-ups*. They give a lift to family meals and are a real lifesaver when unexpected company comes. To name a few: Spiced fruits, specialty soups, main-dish sauces, ice-cream toppings.

6. *Buy a new or different item*. Most families enjoy a surprise, and the way to find out if they like a dish is to serve it. But whether it's a new product or a favorite stand-by, remember: Your supermarket can't stock everything. If you can't find what you want, there's always a substitute—and you may like it better.

Hidden Dividends from Canned Foods

If you're throwing away syrups and liquids from canned fruits and vegetables, you're pouring money down the drain. Save them to use in these ways:

Fruit syrups
- Sweeten raw fruits.
- Mix with other fruit juices for a beverage for breakfast or snacktime.
- Combine with a little sugar, cook about 10 minutes, then serve as a pudding or cake sauce.
- Use for part of the liquid in gelatin salads or desserts.
- Heat and spoon over pancakes or hot cereal.
- Spoon over baked ham or roast pork to glaze top.

Vegetable liquids
- Substitute for part milk in cream soup, white sauce, gravy.
- Use as part of the liquid in tomato aspic or vegetable molds.
- Add to canned or homemade soup.
- Stir into roast-meat drippings when making gravy.

502

How Do Cans Measure Up?

Whether you need just 1 cup—or several—for a recipe, you'll find a size can or jar tailored to your needs, as this chart shows. For easy reference, clip it and affix it to the inside of your cupboard door.

6½ to 8 Ounces (Flat)—About 1 Cup
Popular and familiar flat-shape can, used mostly for tuna, salmon, lobster, and crab meat. Pineapple slices—about 4—come in this size can.

8 Ounces—About 1 Cup
"Buffet" size, perfect for 1 or 2 servings. Available in it are most fruits and vegetables, tomato sauces, specialty products, and dietetic foods.

10½ to 11 Ounces—About 1¼ Cups
Its biggest use is for popular condensed soups, but vegetables, as well as some fruits, meat and fish products also come in this convenient size.

12 Ounces (Vacuum)—About 1½ Cups
Slightly squat in shape, this can holds popular vacuum-pack whole-kernel white and golden corn, and golden corn with peppers and pimientos.

12 Ounces (Tall)—About 1½ Cups
Known best as the "fruit-juice can" because of its wide use for fruit juices and nectars, tomato juice, and plain and mixed vegetable juices.

14 to 16 Ounces—About 1¾ Cups
Baked beans and pork and beans are favorites here. This size is used, too, for spaghetti and macaroni products, cranberry sauces, Spanish rice.

16 to 17 Ounces—About 2 Cups
You'll find many fruits, vegetables, ready-to-serve soups, meats, and specialty products in this size that seems just about right for most families.

20 Ounces—About 2½ Cups
Pineapple slices, pie fillings, fruit juices, some fruits and vegetables and specialties are available in this can. Older cooks know it as the No. 2.

1 Pound, 13 Ounces—About 3½ Cups
For a generous measure of fruits, pumpkin, sauerkraut, regular and Italian tomatoes, ready-to-heat soups, baked beans, buy this thrifty size.

1 Quart, 14 Ounces— About 5¾ Cups
A good budget buy in tomato and mixed vegetable juices, also citrus fruit juices. Cooked small whole chicken, too, comes packed in this convenient size.

HOW TO STORE CANNED FOODS

Canned foods seem to last indefinitely as long as nothing happens to the can to make it leak. And while it's smart to have a well-stocked cupboard, keep moving the oldest products out front to use up first. If you have a basement, store your canned foods there, for they keep best in a moderately cool, dry place. If you are limited to kitchen storage, choose a cupboard as far away from the range as possible. A product stored at 70° will keep twice as long as one stored at 90°.

Q AND A ON CANNED FOODS:

Q. *Where is the best place to store canned foods at home?*

A. In your basement, if it is cool and dry and does not drop to freezing temperature. And it's fun to make your own personal supermarket from an old bookcase or boards placed across bricks for shelves. This gives you plenty of room to arrange your choices in separate groups for quick checking. If you store canned foods in your kitchen, choose a cool dry cabinet away from the range or heat ducts or water pipes.

Q. *How long will canned foods keep?*

A. Almost indefinitely, as long as nothing happens to the can or jar to make it leak. When foods are stored for an extremely long time—particularly, a year or more—they tend to lose color, flavor, and some nutritive value. But even so, they are still wholesome. The best practice is to plan for a complete turnover in your supply at least once a year.

Q. *What happens if canned foods are frozen accidentally?*

A. Freezing may change the texture of some products such as creamed soups, giving them a curdly appearance, but it usually disappears on heating. Otherwise, a single freezing and thawing should not change the contents.

Q. *Does a dented can mean that the food inside is spoiled?*

A. No, as long as the can does not leak. Neither does a rusty can mean what's inside is spoiled. However, if a can leaks or has a bulging top that bounces back when you press it, open it and dispose of the contents where even animals cannot find it.

Q. *My mother was an old-fashioned cook who would never leave food in the can after it was opened. Now I see it done everywhere. Who is right?*

A. Frankly, you couldn't find a safer container for storing opened canned foods than the original sterilized can. Just be sure to cover it, then store in the refrigerator the same as any cooked food.

Q. *Once a can of fruit juice has been opened, I pour it into a glass container. Otherwise, it seems to take on a tinny taste. Is this my imagination?*

A. If you plan to keep the opened can for several days, it's better to transfer the contents to a refrigerator jar. When acid juices stand open for a long time, they tend to dissolve a little of the metal in the can. The juice is still perfectly safe, but it may have the metallic taste that you refer to as tinny.

Q. *Why is there so much liquid in canned fruits and vegetables?*

A. Home canners know the answer to this question, for their experience is the same as that of the commercial manufacturer. First, the fresh product is packed into the can, clear to the top, then liquid is added to fill in the spaces. During processing, the heat always draws out some of the product's natural juices, increasing, of course, the liquid that was put in to start with. Home canners call this "cooking down."

Q. *Why are some canned foods paler than the freshly cooked ones?*

A. In processing, foods must be heated to a certain temperature to make sure they will keep properly. Usually this means longer cooking than for those to be eaten right away.

Q. *Why are fruits canned before they are ripe?*

A. They aren't, really, but as in home canning, fully ripe fruit would soften to mushiness during processing. So that fruit choices for canning will both look and taste their appetizing best, they are picked at the peak of firm ripeness.

Q. *Why do some manufacturers confuse us with fractions of ounces?*

A. To keep prices down for you, manufacturers may use one size can for several different products. Since each may vary in the amount that will fit in the can, and the law requires the label to state the exact weight, here's where the fractions show up.

Q. *Why is a product packed in so many sizes?*

A. Some families need a large size; others, small; and some in between, so manufacturers give you a choice.

COOK TIP

Most of us take a can opener for granted, but once you find the one that works best for you—electric, wall-bracket, or hand model—and cuts

503

a neat trim edge, give it good care. Wipe off the wheels or blades after each using so splashed food will not dry on the gears and clog them. Follow the manufacturer's directions for oiling, if needed, for he knows the best way to keep this important tool in running order.

Some Quick Tricks with Canned Foods

With all of the beforehand work done by the canners, there's time to put your own imaginative touch on a canned-food dish. Here are some sleight-of-hand tricks to dress up plain meals:

· Sauté sliced green onions lightly in butter or margarine; stir into canned *peas.*
· Make an old-fashioned egg-rich corn pudding with *cream-style corn* nipped with liquid red-pepper seasoning.
· Stir canned *sea food*—shrimps, crab, lobster, or tuna—into condensed *vegetable soup* and ready-seasoned *stewed tomatoes* for a quick gumbo.
· Slice chilled canned *corned-beef hash;* heat in the broiler and top with cheese slices for a different "cheese-burger."
· Dice part or all of a can of *luncheon meat* and heat with a can each of condensed *cream of celery* and *beef-vegetable soups* for a hearty chowder.
· Open a can of favorite *beans in tomato sauce;* stir in a few sliced canned *Vienna sausages* and heat.
· Drain canned *salmon* and flake; stir into left-over mashed potatoes with grated onion; shape into cakes; brown.
· Stir canned chopped *ripe olives* into canned *spaghetti sauce* to spoon over cooked spaghetti, noodles, or macaroni.
· Make Danish-style open-face sandwiches with canned *sardines,* sliced hard-cooked egg, and *mayonnaise* or *salad dressing.*
· Heat drained canned *fruit cocktail* in butter or margarine and brown sugar to spoon over ice cream.
· Spoon canned *applesauce* into a buttered pie plate; sprinkle with macaroon crumbs and a dash of cinnamon. Bake until bubbly brown. Serve warm with a splash of cream.

504

WHAT YOU CAN LEARN FROM A LABEL

A wise shopper is a good reader. Sound strange? No, indeed, for while most of us rely on familiar brand names, we are choosy about new items. We compare weight and contents with price before deciding which product best suits our cooking need. All this information, and more, clearly printed on every label, gives us the chance to save where savings count most—at the checkout counter. Below are other tips on how labels help you

Inside facts on the outside

A label gives the brand name of the product, tells who makes it, and what and how much is inside the can. It clearly describes the qualities of the product, and, often, how to prepare or cook it, along with a picture and recipe, or a suggestion for storing after opening. Yes, a label is your best guide to the product that is right for you.

Know what to buy—when

Let's talk about canned tomatoes. . . . Supermarkets stock many varieties in a wide range of sizes. There are: Solid-pack tomatoes, inviting enough to double for a winter salad treat; stewed tomatoes, prepared with seasonings; mostly whole tomatoes, for soups, casseroles; egg-shape Italian tomatoes, ready to turn into all sorts of cooked dishes. In other forms tomatoes are available as juices (both plain and seasoned) and sauces and sauce mixes to heat and serve; also purees and pastes to simmer for a deep rich tomatoey flavor. Quite a list, isn't it? But like other products in a single category, prices as well as uses vary. So read the labels, then choose what best suits your need.

What is a descriptive label?

United States Government law requires every label to carry certain definite information. In addition, food manufacturers like to add these descriptive helps:

1. Exact measure of the number of cups, sizes of pieces, or number of servings.
2. Accurate picture of the color, size, and appearance of what's inside.
3. Directions for using the product, often in a suggested recipe, which may also be pictured.
4. Instructions for handling and storing.
5. Mention of recipe books or other printed information available. When there's enough space, a brief description of how the product is made may be included.

How you can help a manufacturer

Food companies spare no time, effort, or cost to bring you only perfect products, and it pays to let them know when you are pleased or when you have suggestions that might help them improve labeling. And it is only by continually reading and comparing labels that you learn

Recipe . . .

TOMATOES au GRATIN

1 can (16 oz.) tomatoes
2 tablespoons pickle relish
½ cup soft bread crumbs
Salt
Pepper
1 cup grated sharp cheese

Combine tomatoes, pickle relish and bread crumbs. Season to taste. Pour into a shallow baking dish. Sprinkle with cheese. Bake in a moderate oven (350°F) about 30 minutes. Four servings.

TRY tomatoes with celery, onion, okra or corn; scalloped; stewed; with noodles or spaghetti and chicken or seafood; in Spanish rice; cold.

Brand Name

MOSTLY WHOLE   UNIFORMLY RED

TOMATOES

TRACE OF CALCIUM SALT ADDED

MOSTLY WHOLE
UNIFORMLY RED

TOMATOES

TRACE OF CALCIUM SALT
ADDED

CONTENTS . . . . . 1 LB.

Cups . . . . . . About 2
Average Servings . . 4

PACKED BY

A. W. GOODE CO.

ANYWHERE, U. S. A.

---

which you like best, which are most helpful to you.

According to law, every label must honestly tell you (as on the specimen label above):
1. The legal name of the product ("Tomatoes").
2. Name and address of the manufacturer, packer, or distributor ("Packed by A. W. Goode Co., Anywhere, U.S.A.")
3. Exactly what is inside ("Mostly Whole, Uniformly Red Tomatoes"). On some canned fruits and vegetables you will also find information such as "Variety—White or Yellow Corn;" "Style of Pack—Whole, Halves, Diced;" "Packing Medium—Extra-heavy Syrup."
4. Net contents ("Contents . . . 1 lb."). Soon you will see the contents shown on the front as well as side panel.
5. Facts about artificial coloring or flavoring, or chemical preservatives ("Trace of Calcium Salt Added").
6. Ingredients listed in the order of their importance. For example, tomato sauce, Spanish style: "Tomatoes . . . Salt . . . Peppers . . . Spice." Typical exceptions to this ruling are products such as mayonnaise or canned peas, for which Federal specifications have been carefully set.
7. Diet specifications on diet packs—"Packed in water without sugar, and artificaly sweetened with . . . ," in addition to nutritional analysis and calorie count.

●

CANNED MEATS CAN GIVE YOUR BUDGET A BOOST

Guess! How many canned meats do you think your supermarket stocks? 20? 50? The number is nearer 150. Most are cupboard-shelf items

that include everything from deviled ham to whole chicken. Newer are refrigerated canned meats—bacon, spareribs—that need to be kept chilled. Here's how these dependables can help you save:

So thrifty

With versatile canned meats you can count your blessings in many ways. Most important is that every bit you buy is edible. Packers have taken care of trimming away bone, fat, and gristle, so there's no waste. And the meat is all cooked and seasoned, ready to use just as it comes from the can or to turn into family- and party-good dishes. Often you'll find canned meat items on "special" or several for 00¢. Since most take little cupboard space, you win by stocking up and always having the makings of a meat dish on hand.

So good

Just as apple-pie recipes vary from cook to cook, so do the "recipes" for canned meats, but all start with the same Government-inspected high-quality fresh meats with, of course, the same rich protein goodness. As when buying any canned food, brand name is your best guide. And it's smart shopping to read the label, for it will tell you what's in the can, its weight, number of servings, and, many times, give you new recipe ideas.

So quick

Particularly when time flits by, these stand-bys can save a meal from breakfast through dinner—and in mere minutes. Many are main dishes that need heating only. Others are ideal for platters, casseroles, sandwiches, or salads—both hot and cold. In a fancier mood? Choose one you can dress up with cheese or sour-

505

cream sauce and extra seasonings, or even a foreign specialty to bake or serve in a chafing dish. Tip: If you first chill varieties such as chopped ham, beef, pork luncheon meat, or corned beef, you'll find they cut more neatly and in thinner slices, giving you more servings.

So easy to store

Keep unopened cans of meats in a cool dry place, the same as canned fruits and vegetables, and store those that you buy in your supermarket's meat case in your refrigerator. Most canned hams also need refrigeration, so be sure to check the label. Once the cans are opened, cover any that's left, chill, and plan to use within a day or two.

THE MAGIC LAND OF CANNED MEATS

Today's magic land of canned meats ranges all the way from those packed especially for babies to whole hams, colorfully decorated with fruit.

Snacks and spreads

Rating high in popularity for appetizers and canapés or sandwiches are chicken, ham, tongue, and liver spreads; deviled or potted meats; and cocktail franks, meat balls, and sausages.

All-meat main dishes

What variety here! And it pays to get acquainted with them all. You'll find whole hams in weights from one to about 14 pounds, ham portions or slices; picnics; whole or boned and sliced chicken; boned turkey; roast beef; boneless pork loin; sausages; and pork, chopped ham, beef, veal, or corned-beef loaves.

Prepared main dishes

This category seems almost endless, and most are heat-and-eat foods. If beef is your favorite, just look at these choices you have: Corned-beef and roast-beef hash, dried or chipped beef, hamburgers (plain and in sauce), Salisbury steak, beef and gravy or noodles, barbecue beef, meat balls and gravy, beef and dumplings, goulash, chili con carne, and spaghetti or macaroni with meat. Stew fans can pick from these kinds: Beef, lamb, veal, chicken, meatball, or Brunswick. Prefer poultry? Try chicken or turkey à la king, chicken and noodles, chicken fricassee, or chicken and dumplings. And among other selections are ham and lima beans,

506

bacon, scrapple, chop suey, and the always popular franks and baked beans.

Foreign specialties

With about as much fuss as opening a can, you can enjoy favorites from other lands that usually take hours to fix at home. Many supermarkets stock them in their gourmet section and a few to look for are beef stroganoff, chicken cacciatore, chicken tetrazzini, tamales, and ravioli.

●

TRY THESE EASY DRESS-UPS WITH CANNED MEATS

Stir Worcestershire sauce to taste into chicken stew; heat to boiling; spoon into a baking dish. Top with a pastry crust flavored with a smidgen of sage. Bake in hot oven (400°) until golden.

Cut corned-beef hash into thick slices; dip each in flour seasoned with a dash of ground cloves. Brown slowly in hot drippings until crusty, then serve with a spoonful of mayonnaise or salad dressing mixed with prepared horseradish. (One-half cup mayonnaise or salad dressing and 1 tablespoon horseradish is just peppy enough.)

Wrap thin slices of canned ham around spears of drained cooked asparagus; place in a baking dish. Top with your favorite cheese sauce and bake in a moderate oven (350°) until bubbly hot. Nice for a late Sunday breakfast or supper.

Spread hot toast with deviled ham; top each slice with a poached egg and a big spoonful of your favorite cheese sauce or bottled Hollandaise sauce. Serve for breakfast, lunch, or supper.

Mix diced hard-cooked eggs and chopped pimiento into chicken or turkey à la king; heat to boiling. Serve over split hot baking-powder biscuits.

Prepare packaged Spanish-rice mix and place in a baking dish. Arrange Vienna sausages on top; sprinkle all generously with grated Cheddar cheese. Bake in hot oven (400°) 20 minutes, or until bubbly hot and cheese melts.

Dice beef luncheon meat and heat with canned mushrooms in cream sauce seasoned to taste with prepared mustard or curry powder. Serve over toasted English muffins.

Add prepared mustard to taste to meat balls in beef gravy; heat and serve over cooked noodles mixed with chopped parsley.

MEALTIME MAGIC WITH CANNED FOODS

Canned foods have been around so long we simply take them for granted. But for variety, speed, low cost and adaptability, they're hard to beat. Moreover, they can turn mediocre cooks into magicians: open a can of soup and presto! a savory sauce . . . team juicily pink canned shrimps with pineapple chunks, a tart dressing and suddenly! a South Seas sensation. And there's more—much more—in store as the following recipes prove. So—reach for the can opener and open sesame!

Shrimps Hawaiian
Sweet shrimps contrast pleasingly with tangy pineapple in a creamy dressing
Makes 6 servings

2 cans (about 5 ounces each) deveined shrimps
1 can (about 14 ounces) pineapple chunks
1 can (5 ounces) water chestnuts
6 cups broken salad greens
½ cup mayonnaise or salad dressing
¼ cup crumbled Roquefort cheese

1 Drain shrimps. Drain syrup from pineapple chunks into a cup for Step 3. Drain water chestnuts, then chop coarsely.
2 Place salad greens in a large bowl; pile shrimps, pineapple chunks, and water chestnuts in rows on top.
3 Blend 2 tablespoons of the saved pineapple syrup into mayonnaise or salad dressing and cheese in a small bowl; drizzle over salad mixture; toss lightly to mix.

Summer Ham Scallop
For a satisfying meal, serve with a big green salad and crusty bread
Bake at 350° for 1 hour. Makes 8 servings

1 one-pound canned ham
1 package (about 4 ounces) potato chips
2 cans (12 or 16 ounces each) whole-kernel corn
2 cans (1 pound each) small boiled onions, drained

1 cup thinly sliced celery
2 hard-cooked eggs, shelled and diced
¼ cup chopped parsley
4 tablespoons (½ stick) butter or margarine
4 tablespoons all-purpose flour
1 envelope instant beef broth
   OR: 1 beef-flavor bouillon cube
⅛ teaspoon pepper
1 tall can (14½ ounces) evaporated milk

1 Cut ham into ¼-inch-thick slices. Pick out four of the largest center slices and halve each diagonally for garnish; dice remaining.
2 Set aside 8 large potato chips for garnish; crumble remaining coarsely. (There should be about 2 cups.)
3 Drain liquid from corn into a cup; combine corn with onions, diced ham, crumbled potato chips, celery, diced eggs, and parsley in a greased 12-cup baking dish.
4 Melt butter or margarine in a medium-size saucepan; stir in flour, beef broth or bouillon cube, and pepper; cook, stirring constantly, until bubbly.
5 Add enough corn liquid to evaporated milk to make 2 cups; stir into flour mixture in saucepan. Continue cooking and stirring, crushing bouillon cube, if used, with a spoon, until sauce thickens and boils 1 minute. Pour over meat and vegetables; toss lightly with a fork to mix.
6 Arrange ham triangles in a circle on top; tuck saved potato chips between ham slices; cover.
7 Bake in moderate oven (350°) 1 hour, or until sauce is bubbly. Just before serving, garnish with sprigs of parsley, if you wish.

Curried Chicken Salad
Spiced just right for most tastes. Almonds add a nice crunch
Makes 4 servings

¾ cup precooked rice
½ cup chopped red apple
1 can (5 or 6 ounces) boned chicken, cubed
¼ cup toasted slivered almonds
1½ teaspoons grated onion
⅓ cup mayonnaise or salad dressing
2 tablespoons light cream or table cream
1 tablespoon lemon juice
½ teaspoon curry powder
¼ teaspoon salt
¼ teaspoon sugar

1 Cook rice in a small saucepan, following label directions; cool to room temperature. Combine with apple, chicken, almonds, and onion in a medium-size bowl.

507

2 Blend remaining ingredients in a cup; stir into rice mixture; chill. Just before serving, garnish with sliced red apple, if you wish.

Golden Tuna Pie
Refrigerated biscuits are your short-cut helper to its inviting topper
Bake at 425° for 45 minutes. Makes 6 servings

2 cans (1 pound each) lima beans, drained
2 cans (about 7 ounces each) tuna, drained and flaked
1 can (1 pound) stewed tomatoes
1 tablespoon sugar
½ teaspoon Italian seasoning
1 small package refrigerated plain or butter-milk biscuits
2 tablespoons butter or margarine, melted
¼ cup cornmeal

1 Mix lima beans and tuna with tomatoes, sugar, and Italian seasoning in a 6-cup baking dish.
2 Bake in hot oven (425°) 30 minutes, or until bubbly.
3 While tuna mixture bakes, separate the 6 biscuits; cut a hole in center of each with a doughnut cutter. Roll both large and small circles in melted butter or margarine in a pie plate, then in corn meal to coat well. Arrange on top of tuna mixture.
4 Bake 15 minutes longer, or until biscuits are crusty-golden.

Relish Vegetables
Makes 6 servings

1 can (1 pound) mixed vegetables
1 can (1 pound) tomato wedges
¼ teaspoon salt
⅛ teaspoon pepper
½ cup bottled herb-garlic French dressing
½ small green pepper, seeded and diced
1 small onion, peeled and sliced

1 Drain liquids from vegetables and tomato wedges and chill to add to soup another day.

Relish Vegetables toss together zippity-quick.

Place vegetables in the center of a shallow serving dish; arrange tomato wedges around edge. Sprinkle salt and pepper over vegetables; drizzle dressing over all; chill.
2 When ready to serve, garnish with green pepper and onion.

Macaroni-Cheese Chowder, hearty enough for a main dish, goes from can to table in about ten minutes.

Macaroni-Cheese Chowder
Makes 6 servings

1 medium-size onion, chopped (½ cup)
½ cup thinly sliced celery
2 tablespoons butter or margarine
2 cans (15 ounces each) macaroni-and-cheese
1 can (about 1 pound) peas and carrots
1 tall can (14½ ounces) evaporated skim milk
½ cup water
1 teaspoon salt
⅛ teaspoon pepper
½ teaspoon ground marjoram
2 tablespoons chopped parsley

1 Sauté onion and celery in butter or margarine until soft in a large saucepan.
2 Stir in macaroni-and-cheese, peas and carrots and liquid, milk, water, salt, pepper, and marjoram.
3 Heat very slowly, stirring several times, until hot. (Do not boil.)
4 Ladle into a heated tureen or soup bowls; sprinkle with chopped parsley.

Caraway Kraut
Makes 4 servings

5 slices bacon
1 can (1 pound) sauerkraut, drained

508

1 can (1 pound) stewed tomatoes
1 teaspoon sugar
½ teaspoon caraway seeds
¼ teaspoon salt
⅛ teaspoon pepper

1 Cut 2 slices of the bacon into 1-inch pieces. Sauté until crisp in a medium-size frying pan; remove and drain on paper toweling. Sauté remaining 3 slices until almost crisp in same pan, then before removing from pan, roll each slice around the tines of a fork to make a curl; drain on paper toweling. Pour all drippings from pan.
2 Combine sauerkraut, tomatoes and liquid, sugar, caraway seeds, salt, and pepper in frying pan; heat to boiling; cover. Simmer 10 minutes.
3 Stir in bacon pieces; spoon into a heated serving bowl. Garnish with bacon curls and parsley, if you wish.

Green-And-Gold Vegetable Bowl
Sunny carrots and green beans make this bright go-with for a cold-cut platter
Makes 6 servings

1 can (about 1 pound) cut green beans, drained
1 cup sliced celery
2 cans (about 1 pound each) sliced carrots, drained
¼ cup vegetable oil
2 tablespoons lemon juice
1 teaspoon instant minced onion
1 teaspoon dried parsley flakes
1 teaspoon sugar
½ teaspoon salt
Lettuce

1 Toss beans with celery in a small bowl; place carrots in a second bowl. Mix vegetable oil, lemon juice, onion, parsley flakes, sugar, and salt in a cup; drizzle half over carrots and remaining over beans; toss each lightly. Chill to season and blend flavors.
2 Spoon carrot and bean mixtures in separate piles in a lettuce-lined shallow serving bowl. Serve with mayonnaise or salad dressing, if you wish.

Curried Salad Succotash
Makes 8 servings

1 can (12 or 16 ounces) whole-kernel corn
1 can (1 pound) baby lima beans
1 medium-size onion, chopped (½ cup)
½ cup chopped celery
¼ cup chopped green pepper

¼ cup diced pimiento
½ cup firmly packed brown sugar
1 tablespoon curry powder
2 three-inch pieces stick cinnamon, broken
1 teaspoon whole cloves
1 teaspoon celery seeds
1 teaspoon salt
1 cup cider vinegar

1 Drain liquids from corn and lima beans into a 2-cup measure. Combine corn, lima beans, onion, celery, green pepper, and pimiento in a bowl.
2 Combine ½ cup of the vegetable liquid, brown sugar, curry powder, cinnamon, cloves, celery seeds, salt, and vinegar in a medium-size saucepan. Heat, stirring constantly, to boiling; simmer 10 minutes. Strain over vegetable mixture. Cool, then chill overnight to season.

Curried Succotash, another canned quickie.

Ginger-Orange Mold
Makes 6 servings

1 package (3 ounces) lemon-flavor gelatin
½ teaspoon onion powder
¼ teaspoon ground ginger
1 cup boiling water
1 can (11 ounces) mandarin-orange segments
Cold water
1 can (5 ounces) water chestnuts, drained and sliced thin

1 Combine gelatin, onion powder, and ginger in a medium-size bowl; stir in boiling water until gelatin dissolves.
2 Drain syrup from mandarin-orange segments into a 1-cup measure; add cold water to make 1 cup; stir into gelatin mixture. Chill about 45 minutes, or until as thick as unbeaten egg white. Fold in orange segments and water chestnuts; pour into a 4-cup mold. Chill several hours, or until firm.

509

3 When ready to serve, unmold onto a serving plate. Frame base with chicory or curly endive, if you wish.

●

Peach-Cream Cake
Bake at 375° for 15 minutes. Makes 8 servings

1 cup sifted cake flour
1 teaspoon baking powder
¼ teaspoon salt
3 eggs
1 cup sugar
¼ cup water
1 teaspoon vanilla
1 can (1 pound) cling-peach slices
½ cup dairy sour cream
¾ cup currant jelly
1 package fluffy white frosting mix
  Boiling water

1 Grease a baking pan, 15x10x1; line bottom with wax paper; grease paper.
2 Measure flour, baking powder, and salt into a sifter.
3 Beat eggs until foamy in a medium-size bowl; slowly beat in sugar until mixture is thick and fluffy. Stir in the ¼ cup water and vanilla.
4 Sift flour mixture over top; fold in until no streaks of white remain. Spread evenly in prepared pan.
5 Bake in moderate oven (375°) 15 minutes, or until center springs back when lightly pressed with fingertip. Cool in pan on a wire rack 5 minutes. Loosen cake around edges with a knife; invert onto a large wire rack; peel off wax paper. Cool cake completely.
6 While cake cools, drain syrup from peaches into a small bowl and save to add to fruit punch.

Set aside 8 peach slices for garnish; chop remainder and stir into sour cream in a small bowl.
7 Cut cake in half lengthwise, then crosswise to make 4 even pieces. Spread each of three pieces with ¼ cup of the jelly, then ⅓ cup of the peach mixture. Stack layers on a serving plate; top with plain layer. Chill 2 to 3 hours.
8 Prepare frosting mix with boiling water, following label directions; spread over sides and top of cake. Place remaining peach slices across top of cake. Slice crosswise.

Pear Imperatrice
Makes 6 servings

1 can (1 pound, 13 ounces) pear halves
1 container (about 2 ounces) red-cinnamon candies
1 cup cooked regular rice
1½ cups milk
1 envelope unflavored gelatin
¼ cup sugar
3 egg yolks
1 package (2 ounces) whipped topping mix
  Vanilla
2 teaspoons cornstarch

1 Drain syrup from pears into a small saucepan; place pears in a shallow dish.
2 Add cinnamon candies to syrup; heat slowly, stirring several times, until candies melt; pour over pears. Chill, turning several times, at least an hour to tint and season.
3 Combine cooked rice and 1 cup of the milk in a medium-size saucepan. Heat slowly, stirring constantly, until milk is absorbed; remove from heat.
4 Remove all but 3 of the pear halves from syrup; chop coarsely.
5 Mix gelatin and sugar in a medium-size saucepan; beat in ¾ cup of the cinnamon syrup from pears and egg yolks; stir in chopped pears. Heat slowly, stirring constantly, until gelatin dissolves; fold into rice mixture. Chill until completely cold.
6 Prepare topping mix with remaining ½ cup milk and vanilla, following label directions; fold into rice mixture. Spoon into a 4-cup bowl. Chill several hours, or until firm.
7 Drain syrup from remaining pears into a small saucepan. Smooth cornstarch with a little water to a paste in a cup; stir into syrup mixture. Cook, stirring constantly; until sauce thickens and boils 3 minutes; cool.
8 When ready to serve, unmold rice mixtures into a shallow serving bowl. Cut each of the 3 pears in half lengthwise; arrange over rice mold. Spoon sauce over all.

510

Ginger-Orange Mold contains canned mandarin oranges.

LIST OF RECIPES IN VOLUME IV

512